Media Law in Ethiopia

Media Law in Ethiopia

Berihun Adugna Gebeye
Shimels Sisay Belete

This book was originally published as a monograph in the International Encyclopaedia of Laws/Media Law.

Founding Editor: Roger Blanpain
General Editor: Frank Hendrickx
Volume Editors: Peggy Valcke & Eva Lievens

Wolters Kluwer

Published by:
Kluwer Law International B.V.
PO Box 316
2400 AH Alphen aan den Rijn
The Netherlands
E-mail: international-sales@wolterskluwer.com
Website: lrus.wolterskluwer.com

Sold and distributed in North, Central and South America by:
Wolters Kluwer Legal & Regulatory U.S.
7201 McKinney Circle
Frederick, MD 21704
United States of America
Email: customer.service@wolterskluwer.com

Sold and distributed in all other countries by:
Air Business Subscriptions
Rockwood House
Haywards Heath
West Sussex
RH16 3DH
United Kingdom
Email: international-customerservice@wolterskluwer.com

Printed on acid-free paper

ISBN 978-94-035-1330-0

e-Book: ISBN 978-94-035-1370-6
web-PDF: ISBN 978-94-035-1395-9

Printed and bound by CPI Group (UK) Ltd, Croydon, CR0 4YY

The Authors

Berihun Adugna Gebeye is a Doctoral Candidate in Comparative Constitutional Law at the Central European University. He has held visiting research fellow positions at the Centre for Socio-Legal Studies, University of Oxford, UK and the Columbia Law School, Columbia University, USA. He has also been a Global Teaching Fellow at the University of Yangon, Myanmar and a Lecturer in Laws at the Jigjiga University, Ethiopia.

Berihun received his LLB in Laws from Haramaya University, Ethiopia, an LLM in Human Rights Law from Addis Ababa University, Ethiopia, and an LLM in Human Rights with International Justice Specialization from Central European University. His doctoral research is about how the interaction between liberal constitutionalism and indigenous African legal and political systems influence the nature and practice of constitutional government in Africa.

His publications in the field of comparative constitutional law, human rights, legal pluralism, and law and development appeared in the *Journal of Legal Pluralism and Unofficial Law*, *Canadian Journal of African Studies*, *Human Rights Review*, *Vienna Journal on International Constitutional Law*, *Africa Journal of Comparative Constitutional Law*, *Queen Mary Law Journal*, *African Studies Quarterly*, *Journal of Pastoralism*, and *Oromia Law Journal* among others. He presented his research at national and international conferences held at Oxford, Columbia, Harvard, Queen Mary, and the University of Witwatersrand.

Shimels Sisay Belete is a co-founder of the international human rights non-governmental organisation called *Human Rights Matter* based in Berlin, Germany and works as a legal expert for the Organisation. He also teaches at Europa-Universität Viadrina in Frankfurt (Oder), Germany, for the Masters Programme in International Human Rights and Humanitarian Law (LLM) and in the Summer Programme on the European System of Human Rights Protection. He has also held a visiting research fellow position at the Ludwig Boltzmann Institute for Human Rights in Vienna, Austria. He has also worked as a short-term intern at the Federal Republic of

German Parliament: *Bundestag*. Shimels also served as Dean of the School of Law, Head of the Legal Aid Centre, and Lecturer in Laws at Wollo University, Ethiopia.

Shimels received his LLB in Laws from Haramaya University and LLM in Human Rights Law from Addis Ababa University, Ethiopia. He completed his doctoral studies at Europa-Universität Viadrina and has received his Doctoral Degree in Laws (Dr iur). His doctoral research, which is published as a book, critically examines the notion of the right to liberty and security versus counter-terrorism under international law and the discourse within the purview of authoritarian states, and analyses the Ethiopian legal and institutional framework as a case study. Shimels has presented his research papers in different international symposiums and conferences held in Germany and abroad.

Table of Contents

List of Abbreviations

EBA	Ethiopian Broadcasting Authority
EBC	Ethiopian Broadcasting Corporation
EPRDF	Ethiopian People's Revolutionary Democratic Front
ESAT	Ethiopian Satellite Television
FDRE	Federal Democratic Republic of Ethiopia
ICCPR	International Covenant on Civil and Political Rights
OMN	Oromia Media Network

List of Abbreviations

Preface

During the writing of this monograph, Ethiopia has been under a political transition from one of repression to free expression of ideas and views. Accordingly, there is a huge optimism for the operation of free and independent media in Ethiopia. This monograph presents the Ethiopian media law regime to a broader audience and helps Ethiopian policymakers in liberalising the media sector.

Preface

General Introduction

§1. General Background of the Country

I. Political and Legal System of the Country

1. Ethiopia is one of the oldest countries in the world. It is the only African country which successfully resisted European colonialism despite waves of Italian aggression at the end of the nineteenth century and the beginning of the twentieth century. Its history dates back to more than 3,000 years ago. However, Ethiopia received its territorial shape in the current form in the late nineteenth century during the reign of Emperor Menelik II (1844–1913). Its capital Addis Ababa, which means New Flower and was named by Empress Taytu Betul, was established in 1886. In much of its history, Ethiopia was ruled by imperial monarchs. Although Ethiopia adopted its first written constitution in 1931, there were earlier documents of constitutional importance such as the Fetha Negest (The Law of the Kings) and Kibre Mengist. The imperial chapter of Ethiopian history was closed by the overthrow of Emperor Haile Selassie I (1892–1974) in 1974 during the popular revolution. While the Emperor was keen to modernise the country, in particular, through the introduction and expansion of Western education and legal transplantation, his throne could not handle the social unrest and revolution. The military junta known as *Dergue* hijacked the popular revolution and ruled Ethiopia for seventeen years along communist and Marxist ideologies. In this time, gross human rights violations and civil war engulfed the country. In May 1991, the *Dergue* was removed by the Ethiopian People's Revolutionary Democratic Front (EPRDF) – a coalition of ethnic-based liberation movements – and the Eritrean People's Liberation Front after years of armed struggle. The removal of *Dergue* ushered in a new era for Ethiopia. Not only did Ethiopia become a landlocked country with the independence of Eritrea, but a new socio-economic and political order centred on ethnic groups called 'Nations, Nationalities and Peoples' had been set in motion.[1]

2. In July 1991, EPRDF organised a National Conference to facilitate the transition and the exercise of political power in Ethiopia. Out of the conference, a Transitional Period Charter was adopted and a Transitional Government consisting of Council of Representatives and Council of Ministers headed by a Chairperson and supported by a Prime minister was established. The Transitional Charter provided

1. *See* Fasil Nahum, *Constitution for a Nation of Nations: The Ethiopian Prospect* (The Red Sea Press 1997).

the ideals of human rights, democracy, and peace as guiding principles and rules for the Transitional government. In its first article, the Charter adopted the Universal Declaration of Human Rights as a basis for the respect and promotion of human rights in general, and the protection of the freedom of conscience, expression, association and peaceful assembly along with political freedoms related to participation in political parties and activities. Further, it affirmed the right to self-determination of Nations, Nationalities and Peoples. Although the transitional period was supposed to last for two years, it continued for another two years and ended in 1994.

3. Following this was the adoption of the Federal Democratic Republic of Ethiopian (FDRE) Constitution (the Constitution) in 1995. The Constitution established a federal state, mainly along ethnic and linguistic lines, composed of nine regional states, i.e., the state of Tigray, Afar, Amhara, Oromia, Somalia, Benshangul/Gumuz, Southern Nations, Nationalities and Peoples, Gambela and Harari, and two city administrations of Addis Ababa and Dire Dawa. According to the federal arrangement, there are legislative, executive and judicial organs at the federal and regional levels. The federal legislature is composed of the House of Representatives representing the Ethiopian people and the House of Federation representing the various ethnic groups. The House of Federation, the upper house of parliament, is entrusted with constitutional interpretation. In this task, it is supported by the Council of Constitutional Inquiry whose members are legal professionals. The federal executive is composed of a prime minister, deputy prime minister, and council of ministers. The Federal Judiciary consists of the Federal Supreme Court, the Federal High Court, and the Federal First Instance Court. The Federal Supreme Court is the final Court of Appeal on legal matters excluding constitutional matters throughout the federation.

4. Ethiopia is a parliamentary system where the Prime Minister is the head of the government while the President is the head of the state. Unlike the Prime Minister, the President performs ceremonial functions by, for instance, opening the joint sessions of parliament and receiving the credentials of foreign ambassadors and dignitaries, as such the influence of the presidency in the function of the state is negligible. However, the Prime Minister is empowered with enormous executive powers in the operation of the federation. The Prime Minister is elected among members of the House of Peoples' Representatives, the lower house, from a political party or coalition of political parties which have a majority seat. Since 1991, EPRDF has controlled the majority seat in parliament and the premiership. In particular, in the 2010 and 2015 national elections, EPRDF had controlled 99.6% and 100% of the seats in parliament respectively. This turns the multi-party democratic promises of the transition period on its head, as Ethiopia is still a one-party state practically for all intents and purposes, after more than two decades of the federal democratic experiment. The lack of political pluralism coupled with the inability to deliver rule of law, good governance and self-determination have resulted in waves of mass and popular protests, since November 2015 in particular in the Oromia and Amhara regional states. Unable to control the situation by regular law enforcement mechanisms, the Ethiopian government declared a state of emergency twice.[2] While the state of emergency has been lifted and a new prime minister has been appointed, the political situation of the country is still unfolding.

5. The Ethiopian legal system predominantly belongs to the civil law tradition. The substantive and procedural laws of Ethiopia are written. Such writing of laws and transplantation of civil, commercial and penal codes in the 1950s and 1960s, mainly from France, was justified on grounds of certainty, clarity and intelligibility of laws. While the Ethiopian legal system is loyal to the civil law tradition, it did incorporate some aspects of common law tradition recently. This is due to the fact that the decisions of the Federal Supreme Court in its cassation division are binding on lower courts as law. In addition, customary and sharia laws are applicable to personal and family matters based on the consent of the parties. While an enabling legislation for the application of customary law is not enacted, a majority of Ethiopians in particular in rural and peripheral areas rely on customary laws for the dispensation of justice.[3] For the application of sharia law, however, legislation for the establishment of Sharia courts is enacted and they render religiously informed justice for the Muslim community. While the legal system is plural, as it contains customary, statutory and sharia laws, the application and implementation of these laws should not offend the Constitution. If they found to be inconsistent with the Constitution, they will be null and void to the extent of their inconsistency.

II. Geography and Population

6. Ethiopia is a landlocked country located in East Africa, in the part known as the Horn of Africa, bordered by Kenya in the South, Somalia in the South East, Djibouti in the East, South Sudan and Sudan in the West, and Eritrea in the North. With a total area of 1,127,127 square kilometres, the Ethiopian topography ranges from 125 meters below sea level in the Danakil depression in Afar to 4,620 meters above sea level in Ras Dashen in the Semien Mountains. While Ethiopia's topography is largely high plateau, it has deserts along the eastern border, tropical forests in the South, and waves of mountains and plateaus in the North and South East. The Great Rift Valley separates the Western and Eastern part of the country and contains the lakes of Abaya, Chamo, Zway, Shala, Koka, Langano, Abijatta and Awasa which have huge socio-economic and cultural importance to the local people and the country at large. Lake Tana, the source of the Blue Nile, is found in the North. In addition to being the largest lake in Ethiopia, Lake Tana hosts centuries-old churches and monasteries rich in history, architecture and Orthodox Christian spirituality.

---

2. Al Jazeera, *Ethiopia Declares State of Emergency after PM Quits*, https://www.aljazeera.com/news/2018/02/ethiopia-declares-state-emergency-state-media-180216131904605.html (accessed 21 Jun. 2018).
3. *See* Bahru Zewde & Siegfried Pausewang, *Ethiopia: The Challenge of Democracy from Below* (Nordic Africa Institute 2002).

Ethiopia is also endowed with major rivers which pass through its numerous topographies such as the Abay (Blue Nile), Awash, Baro, Omo, Tekkeze, Wabe Shebelle and Genale.

7. Due to Ethiopia's diverse topography, it has four climate regions mainly influenced by altitude. The first is *Dega* where the average temperature is between 10°C and 16°C in the highlands (around 2,500 meters above sea level). The second is *Weina Dega* where the average temperature falls between 16°C and 20°C in highlands (around 1,500–2,500 meters above sea level). The third is *Kolla,* the average temperature there being between 20°C and 30°C in places where the altitude is between 500 and 1,500 meters above sea level. The fourth one is *Bereha* covering deserts whose altitude is below 500 meters above sea level, with an average annual temperature of over 30°C. Ethiopia has four seasons *Kirmet* (summer), *Belg* (autumn), *Bega* (winter) and *Tseday* (spring). Ethiopia recognises thirteen months, the thirteenth month being *pagume* which consists of five or six days, depending on seasons, and comes in between August and September.

8. The population in Ethiopia is 94,352,000, of which 75,188,000 live in rural areas, according to the 2017 report of the Central Statistical Agency of Ethiopia. Composed of more than eighty ethnic and linguistic groups, Ethiopia is indeed a mosaic of people. This population is composed of 34.4% Oromo, 27% Amhara, 6.2% Somali, 6.1% Tigrayian, 4% Sidama, 2.5% Gurage, 2.3% Welaita, 1.7% Hadiya, 1.5% Gamo, 1.3% Gedeo, 1.3 Silte, 1.2% Keffìcho and 8.8% other ethnic and linguistic groups. The languages of these ethnic groups belong to four language families. Among the Semitic languages Amharic, Ge'ez, Gurage, Tigregna and Hareri are the major ones. Amharic is both the working language and widely spoken language of Ethiopia, which is native to the northern and central areas. Ge'ez was once the official language of the Ethiopian state during the Axumite Empire and is still spoken and used in the Ethiopian Orthodox Church. Tigrega is spoken in the north while Gurage and Hareri are spoken in the south and east respectively. The Cushitic languages mainly consist of Oromiffa, Somali and Afar spoken in the western, south western, southern and eastern parts of Ethiopia. Unlike the Semitic and Cushitic languages, the Omotic languages such as Welayita and the Nilo Saharan languages such as the Kunama are spoken by relatively few people in the southern, south western and western lowlands.

9. Agriculture is the backbone of the Ethiopian Economy. The rural population depends for their livelihood on rain-fed agriculture. In the lowlands, pastoralism is the principal means of livelihood. For more than a decade, however, the Ethiopian government has invested in infrastructure, energy, industrialisation and service sectors. Accordingly, the economy has been growing by 11%, making Ethiopia one of the fastest growing countries in the world. As land is owned by the state, the government's development intervention in power production and distribution, road and railway construction, and industrial park establishment among others has created a tension between the government and the people due to displacement. While income inequality is one of the lowest in the world, its growth with the growth of the economy is a development challenge Ethiopia faces. The Ethiopian national currency is called Birr.

III. Social and Cultural Values

10. Ethiopia is a multi-ethnic and multi-lingual country. In spite of this diversity, religion is an important part of Ethiopian life from North to South and from East to West.[4] Among the different religions worshiped in Ethiopia, Orthodox Christianity is the major one. It emerged in the mid-fourth century much hundreds of years earlier than the development of Christianity in Europe. Accordingly, Orthodox Christianity under the Ethiopian Orthodox Tewahido Church is deeply rooted in Ethiopian history, social life and ethics. Orthodox Christianity played a crucial role in the formation of the Ethiopian state and gave the state its unique identity. The distinctive Ethiopian calendar, alphabet and numerical systems are among the many contributions of the Ethiopian Orthodox Church. Orthodox Christianity had been an official state religion until the 1974 revolution where state and religion were separated. Islam is the second dominant religion in Ethiopia. It arrived in Ethiopia in the seventh century. As the case with Orthodox Christianity, Islam is deeply entrenched in the Ethiopian social, cultural and ethical fabrics. Precisely because of this, both religions have peacefully coexisted for centuries. In addition, there are also other traditional religions, such as *Waqe Feta*, practiced in Ethiopia.

11. The family is an important aspect of life in Ethiopia. It includes extended members related through blood in multiple generations. Marriage is a significant part of family life. Both men and women are encouraged to marry and form a family. While early marriage was customary in many parts of the country, the expansion of modern education, massive awareness creation and a legislative prohibition and monitoring have reduced the practice. In addition to the family as a social insurance for its members in the event of need in good and bad times, there are traditional social associations such as *Iquib* and *Idir* which support the orderly life of the society. '*Iquib* is an association established by a small group of people in order to provide substantial rotating funding for members in order to improve their lives and living conditions, while *Idir* is an association established among neighbours or workers to raise funds that will be used during emergencies, such as death within these groups and their families.'[5]

4. *See* Donald N. Levine, *Greater Ethiopia: The Evolution of a Multiethnic Society* (University of Chicago Press 2000).
5. Ayele Bekrie, *Iquib and Idir: Socio-Economic Traditions of the Ethiopians*, http://www.tadias.com/v1n6/OP_2_2003-1.html (accessed 19 Jun. 2018).

§2. THE MEDIA LANDSCAPE

12. A hostile political environment for the functioning of independent media is one of the challenges in Ethiopia. Although there was a normative commitment for freedom of expression in the transitional charter and a robust constitutional recognition of the same, the experiment of independent media has been deteriorating.[6] For a few years after the promulgation of the Constitution, there was a relatively enabling environment for print media. Partly as a result of such a democratic opening for the operation of independence media, the EPRDF faced a total electoral defeat in the capital, Addis Ababa, as well as strong competition in the rest of the country from opposition parties, in particular from the Coalition for Unity and Democracy, in the 2005 national election. Since then, the Ethiopian government has enacted draconian legislation restricting the operation of independent media in the name of fighting terrorism.[7]

13. Although the political environment has not been suitable for the flourishment of media outlets, the constitutional protection and the legislative frameworks for the functioning of the media are promising. Even within the constrained political environment, there are media outlets that inform public debate and channel information. The existence of energetic and vigilant journalists committed to the free expression of ideas and informed public debate, on the one hand, and the growing impact of social media, on the other, an enabling environment for the functioning of independent and responsible media has been created. It is no wonder that the government relaxed the space for independent media as social media became the main source for information but also fake news and disinformation. Moreover, the government media is becoming relatively trustworthy and critical of the government, which is unprecedented. Furthermore, after waves of protest movements, the government is inviting banned Ethiopian media outlets in North America and Europe, such as the Ethiopian Satellite Television and Oromia Media Network (OMN), to operate in Ethiopia.

I. Overview of Media Markets and Main Actors

14. With a population of over 95 million and a fast-developing economy, Ethiopia has a huge potential for media markets. There are both private and publicly owned print and broadcast media. However, most of those print and broadcast media are concentrated in the capital, Addis Ababa. The government-owned *Addis Zemen* and *Ethiopian Herald* magazines have a continuous operation with wider circulation, unlike the private print media. Unlike *Addis Zemen*, *Ethiopian Herald* is

6. *See* Mesenbet Tadeg, *Freedom of Expression and the Media Landscape in Ethiopia: Contemporary Challenges*, 5 *Univ. Balt. J. Media Law Ethics*, 1 (2015).
7. Adem Abebe, *Rule By Law in Ethiopia: Rendering Constitutional Limits on Government Power Nonsensical,* CGHR Working Paper 1 (2012), https://www.repository.cam.ac.uk/bitstream/handle/1810/245111/CGHR_WP_1_2012_Abebe(rev.).pdf?sequence=4 (accessed 20 Apr. 2018).

published in English for a foreign and urban elite consumption. Due to the prevalence of widespread illiteracy and inaccessibility, many Ethiopians living in rural and peripheral areas have limited access to magazines and newspapers.

15. The private print media is concentrated in Addis Ababa. Many of the private print media are published in Amharic. Fortune, Capital and Addis Standard are some of the newspapers that are published in English. The private print media covers topics ranging from entertainment, business, politics, and socio-economic and religious life. Those magazines that focus on entertainment, business and religious life have a longer duration than those that cover socio-economic and political issues.

16. Like the print media, the government-owned broadcast media is the main channel of information, advertisement, and entertainment in Ethiopia. The Ethiopian radio and television have a wider audience both in terms of area coverage and dissemination languages. They transmit programmes in many local languages such as Amharic, Tigrigna, Oromiffa, Somali, and Afari and foreign languages such as English, French and Arabic. While there are FM radio programmes, many of them are located in Addis Ababa, with Sheger FM being the prominent one. Numerous FM radio stations are available in many towns and cities in Ethiopia. Among the private audiovisual media, Fana Broadcasting Corporation has the widest coverage and accessibility. It has radio and television programmes that are transmitted in multiple local languages. Next to the Ethiopian radio and television, Fana radio and television have a wider coverage.

17. There are many print and broadcast media providers who choose to operate from North America and Europe due to the hostile media environment at home. The Ethiopian Satellite Television and the OMN, both transmit in many local languages such as Amharic and Oromiffa, and are the most influential broadcasting media. Precisely because of this, their transmission has been jammed by the Ethiopian government many times. In addition, the Voice of America, Deuchablle, British broadcasting corporation, and special broadcasting service Australia transmit their programmes in Amharic, Oromiffa and Tigrigna. Due to the lack of independent media at home, many people consider these media outlets as more credible.

18. While there is a growing interest to expand the media market after the election of the new Prime Minister Abiy Ahmed in April 2018, a high level of illiteracy, lack of infrastructural development, and a repressive government policy still constrain and limit the media landscape. The main actors in the media sector so far are the government and those affiliated with it. However, there is a profound hope that Ahmed's government will create an enabling environment and market for free and independent media.

19. While the use of social media such as Facebook and Twitter is small compared to the total population, it has been influential in disseminating and sharing information instantly. The growth of citizen journalism and social media platforms diversify the range and nature of information in Ethiopia. As the youth constitutes the majority of the population, social media rather than traditional media is preferred as an easy and inexpensive source of information by this group. Because of this, the government has blocked social media platforms on numerous occasions to contain the fast and widespread flow of information through social media from 2015 to the beginning of 2018.

II. Broadcasting Infrastructure

20. Ethiopian broadcasting infrastructure is operated by the Ethiopian Broadcasting Authority (EBA). The most common means of receiving radio and television broadcasts is through terrestrial, satellite, and cable systems. The EBA is required to set other means of broadcasting services as technology advances.

III. Technological and Economic Developments on the Media Markets

21. Ethiopia is one of the fastest growing economies in sub-Saharan Africa. Its massive infrastructural developments related to, i.e., energy, dams, roads, railways, and education have created more opportunities for the growth of the media market. Not only do these bring a demand from the citizenry to access and disseminate information, they also enable media organisations to operate and communicate more easily with their audiences.

22. Nonetheless, the rising cost of publishing and printing challenges the operation of the print media. Given the smaller circulation of private print media, the price of a magazine or newspaper is a bit expensive. The widespread restriction or repression on the content of private print media has further crippled their operation, even if they are willing to incur huge costs and their customers are willing to pay the price they offer. *Addis Neger* was one of the most popular newspaper in Ethiopia but ceased operation due to the government crackdown. While the increase in the cost of publishing and printing is the government's way of restricting the operation of many private print media, the restriction on content has had the most serious impact.

23. Most of the print media in Ethiopia do not have an online presence. Yet, even for those who have an online presence, the weak Internet connection makes it difficult to access their content. Furthermore, the power interruption is a big challenge for both the production and dissemination of media output. Indeed, Ethiopia is exporting electricity to neighbouring countries such as Djibouti and Sudan and accordingly collecting millions of dollars per month. The power interruptions at home are explained through the inability of the electricity transmission and storage lines to broadcast the power needed for domestic consumption. The government is currently working to improve the capacity and efficiency of these electricity transmission and storage lines.

24. Despite rapid economic growth, Ethiopia still has to eradicate poverty. The rural and the pastoral population have severe limitations in accessing print and television programmes. Many people in rural and pastoral areas have neither the financial capacity nor the technological availability to access television and audiovisual programmes. Radio is the most accessible broadcasting service for this section of the population. Many of them use batteries to run their radios. Due to the frequent power interruption in the cities and towns, listening to radio and television programmes is difficult. Some of the broadcasting media have an online presence. Nonetheless, their online presence does not contain the whole content of their programmes.

§3. Sources of Media Law

25. The sources of Media law in Ethiopia are the Constitution, international law, statutes and case law. The Constitution is the primary source of media law. It recognises freedom of speech and the right of access to information. Furthermore, Article 12 of the Constitution makes accountability and transparency of governments one of its basic principles which makes the existence of free and independent media a necessity.

26. The Constitution also makes international law applicable in Ethiopia with respect to the interpretation and application of human rights. Article 13(2) states that '[t]he fundamental rights and freedoms specified in this Chapter shall be interpreted in a manner conforming to the principles of the Universal Declaration of Human Rights, International Covenants on Human Rights and international instruments adopted by Ethiopia.' Accordingly, international human rights laws related to media are applicable in Ethiopia if adopted. Pursuant to Article 9(4) of the Constitution, all international agreements ratified by Ethiopia are an integral part of the law of the land.

27. Statutes enacted by the federal and regional parliaments are the other sources of media law. In this regard, the Press Proclamation No. 590/2008 and the Broadcasting Proclamation No. 533/2007 are the main statutory sources for media law. However, there are numerous other statutes, regulations, directives and rules on media at the federal and regional levels. *See* paragraph 32 below.

28. While there is no case law on media law so far, decisions of the Federal Supreme Court in its Cassation Division are binding and serve as law.

Part I. Freedom of Speech

29. The constitutional recognition of a person's freedom of opinion and expression dates back to the 1955 Revised Constitution of the Empire of Ethiopia.[8] Article 41 of this Constitution had unequivocally cemented that 'freedom of speech and of the press is guaranteed throughout the empire in accordance with the law.'[9] The successively drafted the Constitution of 1974, which never came into force, also had a dedicated and separate provision under Article 25(i) in recognition of the right.[10] Similarly, the 1987 Constitution of the People's Democratic Republic of Ethiopia, which was formulated based on the *Dergue's* socialist narration of the concept had also incorporated freedom of speech as one of its main values, intriguingly by imposing a positive obligation on the state to provide the necessary material and moral support to exercise this freedom.[11]

30. Indeed, even before the coming into force of the current Constitution in 1995, freedom of speech had been depicted as one of the few pioneering rights which was explicitly enshrined under Article 1 of the Charter of the then Transitional Government of Ethiopia.[12] Setting aside its multifaceted pitfalls, it was also during this transitional period that Proclamation No. 34/92 came into force as a separate legislative framework aiming to abolish press censorship in the exercise and implementation of the right, and granting the right to establish an independent press for the first time in the media history of the country.[13]

31. Currently, the legislative landscape which regulates such a right appears to have been increasingly expanding. Apparently, as is the case with other fundamental rights, the Constitution is earmarked as the most ingenious normative foundation in cementing the main tenets of the person's right to freedom of opinion and expression in the Ethiopian domestic legal setup.[14] This said, a more conceivable

8. Conquering Lion of the Tribe of Judah Haile Selassie I Elect of God, Emperor of Ethiopia, *Revised Constitution of Ethiopia*, adopted and came into force 3 Nov. 1955, Addis Ababa, Ethiopia.
9. *Ibid.*
10. The Draft Constitution of the Empire of Ethiopia, August 1974.
11. The Constitution of the People's Democratic Republic of Ethiopia, Proclamation No. 1 of 1987, Negarit Gazeta, Vol. 47, No. 1, Addis Ababa, 12 Sep. 1987, Art. 47.
12. Peaceful and Democratic Transitional Conference of Ethiopia, *Transitional Period Charter of Ethiopia*, Negarit Gazeta, 50th year, No. 1, Addis Ababa, 22 Jul. 1991, Art. 1(a).
13. Transitional Government of Ethiopia, *A Proclamation to Provide for the Freedom of the Press*, Proclamation No. 34/1992.
14. House of peoples' Representatives, *Federal Democratic Republic of Ethiopian Constitution*, Proclamation No. 1, 1995, Federal Negarit Gazeta, 1st year No. 1 (Addis Ababa, 21 Aug. 1995).

approach in confronting the multifarious issues pertaining to its practical application would demand a comprehensive review of all the relevant proclamations and regulations that have been adopted in the recent-past politico-legal history of the country. This, of course, is notwithstanding the Constitution's immitigable value as a supreme normative standard regarding the content and scope of the right.

32. In this regard, laws such as: the Freedom of the Mass Media and Access to Information Proclamation No. 590/2008 [hereinafter the Press Proclamation];[15] the Broadcasting Service Proclamation No. 533/2007;[16] the Anti-Terrorism Proclamation No. 652/2009;[17] the Revised Political Parties Registration Proclamation No. 573/2008;[18] the Electoral Code of Conduct of Political Parties Proclamation No. 662/2009;[19] the Advertisement Proclamation No. 759/2012;[20] the Computer Crime Proclamation No. 958/2016;[21] the Telecom Fraud Offences Proclamation No. 761/2012;[22] and relevant regulations, as well as the pertinent provisions of the general Revised Criminal Code of Ethiopia[23] need to be punctiliously consulted.

§1. The Constitutional Safeguard to the Right to Freedom of Opinion and Speech

33. As the supreme law of the land, the Constitution bestows the much-needed normative essence of the right in manifold perspectives. As a point of departure, the Constitution under Article 12 demands accountable and transparent governance advanced to the extent that it ensures the people's right to call and question the responsible official for any failure in official duties. This constitutional stand upholds the doctrine of the democratic self-governance theory as one of the most fathomable justifications for the protection of free speech and more of the political speech that criticises government policies, responsible authorities, and institutions at large.

---

15. House of Peoples' Representatives, *Freedom of the Mass Media and Access to Information,* Proclamation No. 590/2008, Federal Negarit Gazeta, 14th year, No. 64 (Addis Ababa, 14 Dec. 2008).
16. House of Peoples' Representatives, *The Broadcasting Service,* Proclamation No. 533/2007, Federal Negarit Gazeta, 13th year, No. 39 (Addis Ababa, 23 Jul. 2007).
17. FDRE House of Peoples' Representatives, *Anti-Terrorism*, Proclamation No. 652/2009, Federal Negarit Gazeta, 15th year, No. 58 (Addis Ababa, 28 Aug. 2009).
18. FDRE House of Peoples' Representatives, *The Revised Political Parties Registration*, Proclamation No. 573/2008, Federal Negarit Gazeta, 14th year, No. 62 (Addis Ababa, 24 Sep. 2008).
19. House of Peoples' Representatives, *Proclamation on the Electoral Code of Conduct for Political Parties*, Proclamation No. 662/2009, Federal Negarit Gazeta, 15th year, No. 8 (Addis Ababa, 28 Aug. 2009).
20. House of Peoples' Representatives, *The Advertisement*, Proclamation No. 759/2012, Federal Negarit Gazeta, 18th year, No. 59 (Addis Ababa, 27 Aug. 2012).
21. House of Peoples' Representatives, *The Computer Crime*, Proclamation No. 958/2016, Federal Negarit Gazeta, 22nd year, No. 83 (Addis Ababa, 7th Jul. 2016).
22. House of Peoples' Representatives, *The Telecom Fraud Offences*, Proclamation No. 761/2012, Federal Negarit Gazeta, 18th year, No. 61 (Addis Ababa, 4 Sep. 2012).
23. House of peoples' Representatives, *The Revised Criminal Code of Federal Democratic Republic of Ethiopia*, Proclamation No. 414/2004 (Addis Ababa, 9 May 2005).

34. Second, Article 10 of this same Constitution concretises the inviolability and inalienability of the fundamental human rights and freedoms that emanate from the nature of mankind, and the duty to respect and ensure their practical observance. It goes without saying that the right to freedom of opinion and speech is such an indispensable right that defines personhood as the most dignified being. This approach further substantiates and instils the autonomy theory which invokes the notion of free opinion and expression as an irreplaceable value that symbolises the inherent independence and equal worth of every person in the society regardless of the different ideas and thoughts reflected on issues of common interest.

35. Third, the Constitution's hospitality declaring all the international agreements ratified by Ethiopia as integral parts of the law of the land also conveys the relevant regional and universal instruments into the domestic legal and jurisprudential setup. Such a constitutional openness to the pertinent international instruments and the jurisprudential developments that deal with the substantive and procedural contents of the right undoubtedly sharpen its conceptual narration and the practical application under the domestic jurisdictional markups. This argument is further reinforced in light of the Constitution's interpretational compatibility standard as clearly stipulated under Article 13(1) of the document. Accordingly, the Constitution has renounced its own supremacy when it comes to the interpretation of the specific provisions on fundamental rights and freedoms – Article 29 of the Constitution which embodies 'the right of thought, opinion, and expression' being one of them – unequivocally providing the requisite of conformity with similar contents as stipulated in the Universal Declaration of Human Rights, international covenants on human rights and international instruments adopted by Ethiopia. In doing so, palpable incompleteness, imprecisions, and irregular articulations one may find in the provisions of the Constitution as well as in other domestic legislation shall be rectified in a manner matching the content and scope of the right as it stands in these international instruments.

36. Apart from these general constitutional principles and rudiments highlighted hitherto, the paramount significance of some of its specific provisions in maintaining the overall constitutional absorbability of the right is worthy of special note. The main examples in this regard include freedom of religion, belief and opinion (Article 27), women's right of participation and consultation in national development policies (Article 35(6)), and the right to vote and to be elected (Article 38). These constitutional rights consolidate the horizon of freedom of speech and opinion, and this, in turn, can lead to the enforcement of other constitutional rights in Ethiopia.

37. Alongside this general constitutional impetus and the broader contextual accolade bequeathed to the right, Article 29 of the Constitution presents the specific normative pillar in defining and establishing the right's content and scope, as well as the legitimate grounds for any intrusion against its full enjoyment. The provision is composited in seven paragraphs articulated as follows:

(1) Everyone has the right to hold opinions without interference.

(2) Everyone has the right to freedom of expression without any interference. This right shall include freedom to seek, receive and impart information and ideas of all kinds, regardless of frontiers, either orally, in writing or in print, in the form of art, or through any media of his choice.
(3) Freedom of the press and other mass media and freedom of artistic creativity is guaranteed. Freedom of the press shall specifically include the following elements:
  (a) Prohibition of any form of censorship.
  (b) Access to information of public interest.
(4) In the interest of the free flow of information, ideas and opinions which are essential to the functioning of a democratic order, the press shall, as an institution, enjoy legal protection to ensure its operational independence and its capacity to entertain diverse opinions.
(5) Any media financed by or under the control of the State shall be operated in a manner ensuring its capacity to entertain diversity in the expression of opinion.
(6) These rights can be limited only through laws which are guided by the principle that freedom of expression and information cannot be limited on account of the content or effect of the point of view expressed. Legal limitations can be laid down in order to protect the well-being of the youth, and the honour and reputation of individuals. Any propaganda for war as well as the public expression of opinion intended to injure human dignity shall be prohibited by law.
(7) Any citizen who violates any legal limitations on the exercise of these rights may be held liable under the law.

To a larger extent, content-wise this provision is portrayed as a direct replica of Article 19 of the International Covenant on Civil and Political Rights (ICCPR). A methodical review of the details would, nonetheless, reveal on the one hand the incompleteness in its substantial formulation, but at the same time, with limitation clauses that would enhance the more generous interpretational approach in maintaining the scope of the protection to the extent of a potentially broader margin. Having this general outlook in mind, the various substantive elements of the right are analysed in the following separate sections.

I. Freedom of Opinion: Article 29(1)

38. Exclusively reading Article 29(1), the private freedom to hold an opinion, the provision appears to have an unqualified guarantee as echoed in the phrase *without any interference*. With this purview, holding and forming one's own opinion is an absolute right that cannot be subjected to any form of intrusion under whatsoever circumstances: be it from the state or horizontally from any private actor. Needless to say, such an uncompromised stand is justified on the ground that the right to have one's own opinion is a purely personal stance that begins and ends only within the realm of the person's mind. In this regard, it can be submitted that the untouchable freedom to hold and form opinion signifies nothing but the complete enjoyment of a person's freedom of thought – a right which is also distinctly cemented under Article 27(1) of the Constitution.

39. On the other hand, Article 29(6) and Article 29(7), which respectively stipulate the general limitation clause and the liability for non-compliance to the limitation, have not exclusively exempted such a right from 'legally prescribed' state interventions. That is the typical textual distinction of this 'catch-all' provision to its counterpart in Article 19(3) of the ICCPR, which unequivocally exempts the right from any form of interference. Given this textual ambiguity, coupled with the generally misguided perception in the national politico-legal setup on 'democratic rights' – i.e., the long-standing portrayal of these rights as entitlements affordable only upon the goodwill of the state and the level of democratic entrenchment – the absolute character of the right doesn't seem unquestionable as it stands in the Ethiopian legal system.

40. The practice of freedom of opinion is not without problems. The first challenge is the question of how to define and determine the exact content and scope of the freedom to hold opinion, and the second is how to distinguish it from freedom of expression and communication. Indeed, freedom of expression has legitimate limitations unlike the freedom to hold opinion. As the Constitution does not provide clear indications how the state enforces freedom to hold opinion, its exact content and scope will be ascertained through constitutional practice.

41. This said, the negative aspect of the obligation requires a state to at least refrain from any form of interference; be it in the form of indoctrination, manipulation, or undue influence over the mindset of a person. As a minimum threshold, an individual should not be coerced, threatened in any form, or influenced by any unauthorised means against his/her expressed or implied will in the course of constructing and holding his/her opinion. The government is also bound by its constitutional duty to protect the citizens' right from horizontal obstruction by private intruders. More perplexing, however, is again the practical disconcertment in striking the balance between (im)permissible daily activities, such as the ever-demanded free flow of information – which in itself is vital in sharpening the individual's informed thoughts – vis-à-vis the need for a careful supervision of private advertisings and propaganda, which might pose undue influence in the formation of the person's opinion. Measures aimed at ensuring non-interference to the person's absolute right to hold and form opinion, may therefore potentially lead to restricting others' freedom of expression.

42. Beyond that, a more fundamentalist approach to the right would also invoke the government's positive obligation to fulfil all the conceivable conditions suitable in fostering the person's conscious and subconscious exposure to varied ideas in the market and enhance the capacity of constructing his/her own thoughts. Such a positive obligation demands the framing of appropriate policies, laws, and institutions that best realise the complementarity of holding and forming an opinion to the free flow of the ideas, for the betterment of mankind and societal coexistence.

43. Notwithstanding these rather ambiguous tenets of the right and the practical uneasiness in its application, to the knowledge of these authors, not a single judicial or constitutional interpretation has been rendered either by ordinary courts or by the House of Federation as a body entrusted to interpret the constitution. Indeed, the right to freedom of opinion and expression is, perhaps, the most neglected and untouched discourse in the case law as evident from the jurisprudential dearth on the subject.

44. Aside the lack of such a formal judicial precedence, three controversial policy and practical measures frequently undertaken by the government can be put forward to demonstrate the extent of the problem centring freedom of opinion in the Ethiopian context. One aspect of the trend is the government's recurring measures of detaining a larger section of the youth – mostly arrested and conveyed in mass to the military and police training camps of the country, as responses in the aftermaths of demonstrations and public rallies – to intensive ideology conversion lessons reportedly aimed at changing the detainee's political opinion.[24] The government claims these programmes merely as rehab and disciplinary training aimed at rectifying those who are misleadingly dragged and participated in what it calls 'illegal demonstrations'.

45. Likewise, EPRDF's absolute monopoly in the use of state-owned media outlets for disseminating its own ideologies, policies, and programmes has been largely criticised for its repressive impact against the flow of differing views. The inevitable detractive consequence of such a cartel has also brought in limbo the boundary between the permissible 'government-public' daily flow of information and impermissible and illegitimate acts of state propaganda, indoctrination, and acts of brainwashing which are all against one's absolute freedom of constructing his/her own well informed personal opinion. This challenge became instinctively visible in the post-2005 politico-legal transition of the country whereby the role of regime in power has been increasingly shifting. As such the EPRDF regime went from one of already displayed hegemonic dominance (ever since its inception in 1991 as a ruling party) to one of absolute control as the sole architect of the entire government under a single party rule. This shift has led to the inseparable conflation of its identity as a 'Party' and its duty as a whole-serving 'Government' and the subsequent functional and institutional fusions in its daily operations. As a consequence, these confusions have been exacerbating the difficulty of confronting its status and its policy perspectives as a Party, given the potential risk of being subjected to its counteractive measures issued by this same Party on its prerogatives as a unilaterally standing government.

---

24. Ethiopian Human Rights Project, *Inhuman Treatments in 'Rehab' Training Concentration Camps*. Available at: http://ehrp.org/inhuman-treatments-in-rehab-training-concentration-camps/ (accessed 3 Jan. 2018).

46. Setting aside the routine misplacements of party programmes and missions in the day-to-day functioning of the civil or public service, the direct influence of the Party – shielding under its capacity as a ruling government – in shaping and brainwashing the political mindset of the youth has also become an increasingly noticeable phenomenon in higher education institutions. This trend can be evident from the official assignment of Party focal persons in every public university of the country with mandates such as: mobilising and organising the Party's base within the university community of students and staff; shrivelling and surveillance of those who are deemed to have differing views and thoughts; and watchdogging the university leadership and its fidelity in implementing policies and programmes. No other Party has access to similar official arrangements. An additional example in this regard could be the government's implementation of the annual mandatory training conventions and meetings organised in all public universities before the beginning of the semester and held under the tutorship of the Party's political figures and *cadres* (architects and voices of EPRDF ideologies, policies, and strategies) to which every university student and staff are obliged to take part. While the government justifies these measures as awareness creation sessions on policies and strategies to ensure the peaceful teaching-learning environment, critics on the other hand revile these unwarranted interventions as violations to the constitutional prohibition of embroiling education and educational institutions based on political partisanship, which is clearly stipulated under Article 90(2) of the Constitution. Above all, what is at stake is the fact that no mind constructs a thought of its own in a vacuum. Hence, government actions of tabling its own agendas in academic institutions as channels of reaching the most influential and educated section of the society, while at the same time blocking and jamming other alternative views cannot be neglected as a mere ordinary facet of governance, least on its inexcusable impact in diminishing the person's choice of ideas in the pursuit of forming his/her own opinion mainly when it comes to some critical issues of common national or public interest.

II. Freedom of Expression: Article 29(2)

47. In an even more generous articulation compared to that of Article 19(2) of ICCPR, paragraph 2 of Article 29 of the Constitution states on the right to freedom of expression that: 'everyone has the right to freedom of expression without any interference'. Two distinctive features can be drawn from such a firmly stipulated postulation. First, the phrase 'everyone *has* […]' – which is more straightforward than that of 'the request-based' approach adopted in the ICCPR with the phrase 'everyone *shall have* […]' – dictates the indispensable nature of the right and the role of the law in the pursuit of ensuring its safeguard. That is, the person's freedom of expression is not a right that the law has granted the individual upon the goodwill of the law maker. It is rather a fundamentally irrefutable entitlement that the law should fully recognise the right as defining chore of mankind *ipso facto* and uphold its enforcement. Second, as it can be construed from the term 'any', the extent of the prohibition of the interference against the enjoyment of the right appears to be steadier. Hence the prohibition is both vertical – with the state as a primary duty bearer – and horizontal, which also demands protection against private intruders.

48. It goes without saying that freedom of expression cannot literarily be hustled just as the freedom 'to speak', 'to write', or 'to paint'. It is rather a full-fledged package embedding, on the one hand, all the means and methods propelling the person's potential and capacity in the exercise of the right, and on the other, his or her access to reach out the audience in the competitive market of ideas. That is why the right includes the freedom to seek, to receive, and then to impart information and ideas of all kinds in the manner and with the format that suits the person.

49. Most importantly, as stressed in phrases such as: *all kinds*, and *regardless of frontiers*, the scope of the right cannot be conditioned upon the nature or the positional audacity of the information or the idea. Accordingly, every type of opinion or information – be it subjective or neutral/objective; political, social, cultural, artistic, or commercial; critical or supportive; societal or individual, etc. – shall be protected regardless of its acceptance or denunciation by the mainstream. This entails that ideas, even those containing undesirable content, cannot be blocked merely through a restrictive interpretation of the scope of the right, except those legitimately debarred in light of the permissible grounds explicitly provided under Article 29(6) of the Constitution itself.

50. Aiming to avoid unwarranted and premature interventions against the full enjoyment of the right, the Constitution has also prohibited any form of censorship. The right to freedom of political expression is one of the very crucial aspects of the right, while also being the most infringed aspect by far. In view of its vivacity for the better utilisation of every other right, ensuring the person's right to political freedom of expression demands the broadest and the thickest possible margin in defining its scope and content.

51. Alongside its substantial content, the Constitution has also reverberated the same approach adopted in the ICCPR when it comes to the manner or the forms of imparting ideas or information as manifestations to the full enjoyment of the right. In this regard, the choice as to the form and means of communications is left open to the discretion of the right holder. Hence it can be orally through speech; in writing through printed or electronic formats; in any artistic form through paintings, music, theatre, movie, etc. or through any other media outlet of his/her preference.

52. One notable aspect which lacks clarity at this juncture is the exact obligation of the state as a primary duty bearer in realising the person's freedom of choosing the form of communication. Is it merely the negative obligation to abstain from intervening over the person's choice of the apposite communicative form or does it also entail the positive duty of providing and granting access to those alternatives? In the contemporary media landscape of Ethiopia where both the electronic media and the printing companies are controlled under the monopoly of government ownership, it would be nonsensical if one is to construe the nature of the duty narrowly from the negative non-interference context.

53. The state not only has a duty to abstain from interference but also carries a positive obligation to ensure the exercise of freedom of expression. Within the constitutional limitations, individuals are at liberty to express their ideas and opinions in the way they want and by a means they choose. As a matter of practice, however, the government controls the big printing and publishing companies and consequently controls how and when individual's freedom of expression has to be communicated. This is evident in the repeated grievances and complaints of the private press houses, newspapers, and magazines. Obviously, this goes counter to the state's constitutional duty to enforce freedom of expression.

III. Freedom to Seek and Access Information

54. As an inimitable leeway in advancing a person's prospects and capacity of constructing substantially well-founded and titivated contemplations, the freedom to seek and access relevant information, as well as the practical enforcement thereof, must be placed at the centre of the right. It does not simply imply the gathering of what is offered as a passive recipient; rather it is the right to actively demand the generally accessible information, in line with the textual spirit of Article 29(2) of the Constitution. Such a broad interpretation promotes a vibrant and engaging societal demand in obtaining and filtering the credibility of information. Above all, it fosters the culture of well-adjudged decision making in all aspects of public affairs.

55. As the freedom to seek and access information is not an absolute right, the legislator allows for the justification of violations on grounds such as protecting private data or privacy of another person. Apart from that, a person's freedom to seek information should in no way be infringed by the state's intervention against the pursuit of generally accessible information. This is the negative aspect of the state's obligation in respecting the person's freedom of information. In light of this, restrictive measures, such as: denying the private press from accessing and attending live press conferences; prohibiting or destructing live coverage, recording, and documenting of violent security measures in demonstrations and public rallies; as well as refusals to grant access to and documenting parliamentary debates or other governmental forums, constitute clear violations of a person's freedom to information.

56. On the other hand, the answer to the question of whether this right also imposes a positive obligation on the state to come up with measures facilitating the person's entitlement to receive information appears to depend on the circumstances of the case. To a greater extent, the government alongside its policies, strategies, laws, and institutional architectures is arguably the primary headline of daily societal dialogue. Accordingly, at least citizens' right to seek and receive information about the circadian functioning of the government in the public administration would demand a transparent communication channel that is easily accessible by everyone. Most importantly, to improve the functioning of the media, an equally privileged treatment in the enjoyment of the right to information on matters of public interest is necessary. Moreover, ensuring and protecting the individual's full enjoyment of the right from obstructions by other private intruders (horizontal interventions) is another typical manifestation of the state's positive obligation in regards to a person's right to seek and access information.

IV. Limitations on Freedom of Expression: Grounds, Procedures and Consequences

57. Intriguingly, a careful reading of Article 29(6) indicates that the focal point of the text is more of dictating the restrictive nature and margin of the legitimate grounds for limitations themselves. This can be inferred from the introductory part of the text which stresses that: 'the rights can be limited *only through laws which are guided by the principle that freedom of expression and information cannot be limited on account of the content or effect of the point of view expressed*'. The paragraph starts by cementing the importance of limiting the limitation clauses themselves through an unambiguous exclusionary principle outlawing any content or effect-based approach in justifying the necessity of the interference. Accordingly, a mere enactment of a law aimed at restricting the exercise of the right to freedom of expression is not sufficient in and of itself. Instead, the restrictive law itself should meet the criteria that it is framed with a content and in a manner that does not result in the limitation of the exercise of freedom of expression merely on the grounds of the substance and/or the effect of the view reflected.

58. Within this principal framework, three specific purposes are expressly stated under Article 29(6) as permissible grounds for justifying restrictions to the right to freedom of expression: protecting the well-being of the youth; protecting the honour and reputation of individuals; and restrictions aimed at the prohibition of propaganda for war and injuries to human dignity. In contrast to the scope of its counterpart Article 19(3) ICCPR, it can be submitted that these grounds are articulated in a substantially narrower context. For that matter, nowhere in the FDRE Constitution are the more controversial grounds for limitation, such as the protection of national security or of public order (*ordre public*), explicitly mentioned as permissible justifications. Nor is the protection of public health specifically stipulated as one of the legitimate grounds to be invoked in justifying restrictions on freedom of expression. The use of some specific terms such as, 'the youth' instead of 'the general public', and 'individuals' rather than the whole-catching subject 'others' – a term which may also include legal entities other than individual human beings – would also portray the intended restrictive approach in the course of interpreting and applying these permissible grounds while justifying the various modalities of interventions to the right.

59. On the other hand, it is also worthy of noting the palpable deficiencies of the text of the limitation clause that would exacerbate its abusive and arbitrary application. One major challenge is the very subjective and ambiguous nature of some of the terms used in defining the scope of the legitimate actions backing the restriction. For instance, what does *the well-being of the youth* mean? What constitutes an act to have caused injury to human dignity? Would that mean the prohibition of national, racial, religious or ethnic hatred that may lead to the provocation of discrimination and hostility, as a reference to the prohibition provided under Article 20 of the ICCPR?

60. Above all, the Constitution does not unequivocally require the most indispensable elements of necessity and proportionality as testing requisites while gauging the propensity of the measures. In fact, as a constitutional proviso expectedly subjected to generality in its articulation, the drafters would not have succeeded in formulating a full-fledged and self-executive limitation clause. Hence, addressing these imprecisions would demand a careful and objective assessment of each scenario on a case-by-case base in accordance to the circumstances of its own settings.

61. Having in mind these discrepancies and in view of minimising their against the practical efficacy of the right, the constitutionally permissible grounds and procedures behind every measure of restricting the person's right to freedom of expression and information must be precisely determined in such a manner fulfilling the conditions that: (i) the measure must be backed by a law enacted by the opposite law making body of the country; (ii) it must be justified on the ground of one of the constitutionally listed permissible purposes; (iii) it must be necessary and proportional in light of the intended purpose to be achieved vis-à-vis the damages such a measure would cause to the fundamental tenets of the right in maintaining the free flow of diversified ideas in the market and the resultant benefits both to the individual and the public at large. Most importantly, as a provision containing a limitation against the full enjoyment of the right, Article 29(6) has to be interpreted narrowly, sticking to the literal meaning of the wording in the text, pursuant to the fundamental interpretational rule which prevents any invocation of restrictions or obligations through interpretational inference or analogy.

62. Once the grounds are found to be legitimate, Article 29(7) provides that non-compliance to the restrictions in the exercise of the right would result in legal liability as a consequence. Indeed, most of the measures are deemed preventive or prohibitive as they are pre-emptively aimed at directly or indirectly controlling and banning some mediums of exercising freedom of expression rather than forthrightly targeting the person. Some of the measures in this context include confiscation or forfeiture of printed or electronically produced works, prohibiting the actual dissemination or direct performance of works such as speeches to the audience, theatres and music play, or talk shows. Hence, the legitimacy of these measures has to be methodically assessed in pursuance to the aforementioned conditions.

63. The other consequential aspects of the restrictions are retributive in a sense that the author will be held responsible either in criminal or in civil proceedings, for deeds carried out in the course of exercising the right to freedom of expression and that are deemed in violation of the legitimate restrictions. In this regard, individuals such as authors, journalists, bloggers, editors, publishers, owners of media companies, and political figures are the ones most targeted and subjected to criminal and/or civil punishments depending on the gravity and the nature of the alleged infringement.

§2. Freedom of the Press and Mass Media

64. Not only is freedom of expression and information a substantive right of the individual person, the Constitutional provisions in Article 29(3–5) have also guaranteed the institutional freedom of the press and mass media modalities, including that of artistic works. In particular, the prohibition of any form of censorship and access to information of public interest are deep-seated as typical components of the press freedom.

65. Most importantly, anchoring its irreplaceable value in maintaining the free flow of information, ideas, and opinions that are indispensable in the proper functioning of a democratic order, the Constitution has unambiguously commended the full legal protection to the institutional and operational independence of the press. Furthermore, the need to ensure the capacity and hospitality of the press to entertain diverse opinions is empathically painted. These requirements are applicable to all the press and media outlets regardless of their ownership status either as a private or as a state-owned institution.

66. The Constitution does not prohibit state control or ownership of the press or the media. Article 29(5) demands, however, that any media under a financial or operational control of the government should be functioning as a convivial platform to all differing opinions. That includes ideas and opinions severely critical of the government and its policies, programmes, strategies, and institutions as well as the authorities in their capacity as holders of public office. Accordingly, the State's ownership, financial and administrative control does not give the government an absolute discretion of filtering, intimidating or repressing critics of the regime in power.

67. Minding the afore-highlighted general constitutional stands on the various aspects of the freedom of speech and opinion, the section to follow provides a non-exhaustive review of other pertinent laws that are of paramount importance in regulating the practical observance of the right and the compatibility of the interventions by the concerned authorities.

§3. Ordinary Legislation Aimed at Limiting Freedom of Expression

68. It must be noted from the outset that issues of constitutional interpretation and adjudication, including on the Bill of Rights, belongs to the House of Federation, the upper house of parliament. The House of Federation is a political body constituted of representatives of ethnic groups. Due to its political nature, it is difficult to maintain that the House of Federation will be an independent arbiter in the enjoyment of constitutional rights. This is particularly true for the freedom of speech and opinion when it concerns criticism towards the government. However, with respect to the enforcement of legislation, ordinary courts assume jurisdiction. Considering this, legislation which has a direct or indirect impact on freedom of speech and opinion will be litigated in ordinary courts. If these courts find that there is a constitutionality issue, they will refer it to the House of Federation for disposition. As a result, litigation related to freedom of speech and opinion can be made in both ordinary courts and at the House of Federation.

69. As to the freedom of expression, there is no full-fledged and comprehensive national statute that regulates the A–Z aspects of the subject. Hence, one may have to delve into a multitude of proclamations and regulations that contain provisions envisioned to impose limitations on the right in a particular context. Aiming to take a breakthrough of such an attempt, a non-exhaustive analysis of the relevant legislation of the country is presented in what follows.

I. The Ethiopian Criminal Code: Punitive Aspects of Restriction on Freedom of Expression

70. Perhaps, as the most imperative legislative backup in the enforcement of the limits to freedom of expression and mass media rights, the Criminal Code also contains provisions directly relevant and applicable to the various contentious issues on the subject. Chief among these principles is the section under the general part of the Code (Articles 42–47), which restates the principles and regulates the liability of crimes committed through the media and the specific consequential criminal liabilities of authors, originators or publishers up on conviction. As a point of departure, Article 42 contemplates to define the purpose, the means and the potential targets of the crimes relating to the mass media. Accordingly, whereas the purpose of criminalising some conducts is to ensure freedom of expression while preventing abuse of the right – against the honour of other persons, public or private safety, or any other legal right protected by criminal law – newspapers, books, leaflets, journals, posters, pictures, cinemas, radio or television broadcasting or any other modalities of mass media are cited as typical means of committing the offences.

71. Article 43, on the other hand, identifies the principal offenders of the crime. Holding the primary criminal responsibility on the editor-in-chief of the periodical, other actors namely: the publisher, the printer, the disseminator, or the importer of periodicals published abroad are also respectively held accountable according to the circumstances of the case. More specifically, an author, a contributor, or a publisher of the product published or diffused through mass media are deemed criminally liable either as principal offenders, instigators, or as accomplices in the commission of the crimes prescribed in the Code as: 'armed rising or civil war (Article 240); treason (Articles. 248-250); espionage (Article 252); attempted incitement and assistance (Article 255); provocation and preparation (Article 257); crimes against humanity (Articles 269—274); incitement to disregard military order (Article 332);

disclosure of military secrets (Article 336); breaches of military and official secrecy (Article 396 and 397); inciting the public through false rumours (Article 486(b)); or the deliberate disregard for an obligation to maintain secrecy specified by law'.

72. Aside from this general criminal liability, the Special Part of the Criminal Code has also embodied plenty of provisions aimed at enforcing the retributive consequences of alleged abuses in the exercise of the freedom of expression and opinion. In this regard, the crimes proscribed include: the crime of abusing, insulting, defaming, or slandering the State in public (Article 244(1)); the crime of provocation (Article 257(a)); crime of slander and malicious propaganda against a foreign State (Article 261(a)); insults to foreign state (Article 264); insults or abuses to official emblems of foreign states (Article 265); and insults to interstate institutions (Article 266). Furthermore, provocation of crimes in violation of public international law (Article 274(a)), which includes Genocide, crimes against humanity and war crimes, is also verboten by the Code. Likewise, the provisions dealing with crimes in breach of secrecy against public interest (Articles 396–401); disclosures in breach of secrecy of proceedings (Article 450); and publication of inaccurate and forbidden reports of proceedings (Article 451); and publishing or spreading news, a note, précis, a criticism, a report or a pamphlet, which is adjudged to be inaccurate or tendentious (Article 457), have also a huge stake in the practical aspect of governing the criminal consequences of alleged breaches to the limitations imposed on freedom of expression and the free imparting of ideas.

73. Besides, Articles 485 and 486 of the Code respectively criminalise the most contentious acts of spreading alarm to the public and the crime of inciting the public through false rumours. What is more disgruntling and fallacious about Article 486 is its impact in depicting the government and its authorities as 'untouchable' entities, the daily functions of which cannot be subjected to the naturally inevitable media and public rumours. Such a broader and subjectively construed protection to the government and its authorities shifts and imposes the burden of proving allegations on the public, rather than on the specifically concerned organ of the State. This shift would inherently collide with the very essence of the right to freedom of expression, and the role that the media is ought to serve towards ensuring the utmost level of transparency in every functioning of the government through effective public scrutiny.

74. In one prominent case, veteran journalist *Temesgen Desalegn* was charged and convicted on his role as an author and as chief editor of the then periodical gazette called '*Fitih*' (Justice).[25] As grounds for the first count of the criminal charge, the ideas reflected in the two of his Articles published on the periodical were adjudged to have contained messages constituting an offence of public provocation for the commission of a crime of outrages against the Constitution and the constitutional order, and hence in breach of Articles 43(1) and 257(a) of the Criminal Code. Content-wise, however, the defendant – underlining the oppressive nature of

25. *Federal Central Prosecutor v. Temesgen Desalegn*, Ministry of Justice, Prosecutor File No. 00/076/04, Federal Police File No. 8 463/04, date 2/12/04 E.C.

the current regime; highlighting the past and present resilient and heroic movements of the Ethiopian youth against repressions and their fearless hunger for change – had put forward his analytical prediction of whether the then political situation in Ethiopia had been igniting for similar movements like the *Arab Spring* of its own, and the peaceful engagement of the youth assuming the leading role. Then, the second count of the charge accused the defendant on a serious of pieces of opinions contributed by another author but on his capacity as chief editor, for having committed a crime of defaming and slandering of the government allegedly in violation of Article 244 of the Code. Finally, the third count of the charge brought against the defendant invoked Article 486(a) of the Code and claimed that one of his Article published in the gazette – which revealed the intervention of the government in both Orthodox and Muslim religious hierarchies – constituted a crime of inciting the public through false rumours.

75. Apart from these 'government-protectionist' offences, the Criminal Code also prescribes other speech-related conducts, the purpose of which is regulating the horizontal impact of abuses in the exercise of the right against the interest of another individual, a judicial person or the general public. The typical speech-related misdemeanours in this context are generally categorised in the Code within the crimes against honour (Articles 607–619), and the crimes tending to corrupt morals and the family.

76. The traditionally known offence in the first category is the crime of defamation and calumny as stipulated under Article 613 of the Criminal Code. Also, as per Article 615 of the Code, an act of directly addressing the person, referring and offending in his honour by insult, outrages him by gesture or in any other manner is criminalised as insulting and outrage behaviour. By the same token, as offences to public morality, the Code also penalises acts of obscene or indecent publications (Article 640); obscene or indecent performances; and indecent publicity and advertisements (Article 643).

II. Defamation under the Civil Code: Extra-Contractual Liability

77. Revealingly, the offence of defamation results in not only criminal liability but also a civil action in the form of extra-contractual responsibility pursuant to the relevant provisions of the Civil Code under the sections of tort liabilities arising from offences. The pertinent provisions to this effect are the principle Article 2028 along with the specific rules enshrined under Articles 2044–2049 of the Civil Code.

78. Article 2044 defines what constitutes an offence of defamation, in order for the author to be held accountable and make good of the damages he/she caused to the victim. Accordingly, for the purpose of such a tort-based liability:

> A person commits an offence where by his words, his writings or by any other means he acts in such a way as to make another living person detestable, contemptible or ridiculous and to jeopardize his credit, his reputation or his future.

From the definition, there are certain elements worthy of special note. The first issue relates to the potential victim protected by the definition. As clearly indicated, only a living individual person, can invoke a defamatory action against the author. Certainly, neither a government institution nor an authority in their official capacity is protected under this provision. Second, the purpose of the defamatory acts – be it in words, writings or in any other means – which are deemed as detestable, contemptible or ridiculous must have the impact of jeopardising the honour, credit and future of the victim. As a tort liability, establishing the criminal intent of the author may not, in principle be required, and this is clearly stipulated under Article 2045(1) of the Code. This being the rule, however, the fact that the author had no intention of referring to such utterances or writings to any particular person would suffice to rebut the claim of defamation.

79. More intriguing are the exceptions under which no act of speech or writing or utterance would constitute an offence of defamation for the purpose of adjudging the issue of extra-contractual liability of the author. One typical scenario is expressing opinions on matters of public interest. In this regard, as provided under Article 2046 of the Code, notwithstanding that the opinion may inflict injury on another by bringing him/her under public scrutiny, the author is not deemed to have committed the offence of defamation unless he has made charges against the plaintiff, which to his certain knowledge are false. Perhaps on similar grounds in prioritising and ultimately protecting matters of public interest, the Code has also granted special immunity to speeches and utterances made in parliamentary debates and in the course of legal proceedings.

80. The other ground for exemption from a tort-based liability for alleged defamation claims is the truthfulness of the allegation advocated by the author. In light of this, even if the act may not be covered under the subject of matters of public interest – or in other words, even if it relates to the private matters of the alleged victim – no defamatory offence is deemed to have been committed by the author if he/she proves the truthfulness of the allegations, and that he/she had not acted solely to injure the plaintiff. Apart from that, at times, even if a defamatory act might have been committed but with no intent to injure or without gross negligence, Article 2049 imposes no liability, instead imposing that an immediate publication of a withdrawal and apology at the request of the plaintiff would suffice to rectify the damage.

81. What can be deduced from the afore-cited provisions of the Civil Code is the fact that not only in the criminal cases whereby a stringent standard and burden of proof is required in order for the person to be held criminally liable based upon the criminal intent, the law has provided the maximum protection on the person's freedom of opinion and expression even against the civil actions that may arise on claims of defamatory speeches leading to tort-based liabilities.

III. Freedom of the Mass Media and Access to Information Proclamation No. 590/2008

82. Also called as the 'press law', Proclamation No. 590/2008 reiterates, under Articles 4, 11, and 12, the constitutional freedom of the mass media. It also restates the prohibition of censorship and administrative measures that impair the proper exercising of this freedom in fulfilling the much-needed public function of the media in seeking, receiving, and imparting news or information; as a platform to express opinion and criticism on various issues; and as a modality of ensuring participation in the process of forming public opinion.

83. This said, the Proclamation is highly criticised mainly on three fundamental grounds that are deemed to have undermined the liberally postulated constitutional freedom of the press. The first critique relates to the complicated, bureaucratic, and clumsy procedures that journalists have to follow in order to seek and get access to information of public interest from government offices. For that matter, a textual reading of Article 14 and Articles 31–34 of the Proclamation would reveal the lengthy nature of the process which might take up to three months' period in order to get final decision regarding the delay or refusal of the request. Second, the discretion in determining the relevancy and urgency or otherwise nature of the requested information, and the possibility for disclosure or the need to maintain its confidentiality is solely vested in the hands of the public relation officer of each government office. Hence, the public's right to know timely information rests exclusively on the personal dispensation of the government-employed officer. The very subjective character of the legitimate reasons that may be invoked as possible justifications for the delay, or for the total denial of the demanded information would exacerbate the potential abuse of such a mandate. Indeed, notwithstanding the Proclamation's demand for the criminal liability of any person who intentionally denies the right to access to information – i.e., by destroying, damaging, altering, concealing, or by falsifying a record – for a maximum of up to two years' imprisonment or to a fine, the genuine efficacy of pursuing such accountability appears practically unachievable in light of the generously crafted principle provided under Article 39(1) which exempts the person from any criminal or civil liability for anything done in good faith in the exercise of his/her power.

84. The much-contested discrepancy relates to the wider margin for exemption from disclosure, of public information based on the *ipse dixit* decisions for its confidentiality. To that end, almost one-third of the provisions of the Proclamation (Articles 15–35) is dedicated to the listing of information or documents, in relation to which the public's right to access may partially or fully be impeded, and the procedures to be sought in challenging decisions resulting in such an effect. While the exclusion of some of the information – especially those aimed at ensuring the privacy and vested interest of the third party – appears logical within the ambits of the constitutionally recognised limitations to the right, the other exemptions remain controversial as unwarranted toolkits prompting government secrecy in violation of the constitutional principle of transparency in the conduct of public affairs. Typical examples in this regard are exemptions from public access of cabinet documents, commercial activities of public bodies, and operations of public bodies as stipulated respectively under Articles 24–26 of the Proclamation.

85. The other interventionist aspect pertains to Article 42 of the Proclamation, which entrusts the public prosecutor the power to impound and confiscate periodicals or books and prevent their dissemination on the ground of rather the very volatile issue of national security. Given the politically sensitive and subjective nature of the term, the Proclamation has left an uncharted discretion which may have a diminishing effect against the right to freedom of expression and opinion. Moreover, as clearly stipulated under Article 42(4(a)), the measure of impounding or confiscation of the material adjudged to have covered illegal content may then be followed by initiation of criminal charges against the author and/or the editor or the publisher. Apart from that, the list of financial penalties as set out under Article 45 – ranging from the minimum 15,000 Ethiopian Birr that extends up to the maximum 200,000 Ethiopian Birr – as fines upon failures to comply with the various requirements and restrictions imposed by the Proclamation are also largely considered disproportional in light of the economic capacity of actors involved in the media market and particularly those in journalistic profession.

86. Generally, the foregoing ambiguous mandates backing these kinds of measures may implicate the de facto legitimisation of the constitutionally prohibited censorship. Also worrying, as is often the case, is the fear these actions have the inexorable repercussion of compelling authors, editors, and publishers to get into fright-based self-censorship (or 'chilling effect'), which spoils the ever-demanded free flow of diversified ideas in the society.

IV. The Anti-Terrorism Proclamation No. 652/2009

87. Of the most controversial legislation in this regard is the Anti-Terrorism Proclamation No. 652/2009 of the country. Article 6 of the Proclamation proscribes encouragement to terrorism articulating the elements of the crime in the most elusive manner stating:

> Whosoever publishes or causes the publication of a statement that is *likely to be understood by some or all of the members of the public* to whom it is published as *a direct or indirect encouragement or other inducement* to them to the commission or preparation or instigation of an *act of terrorism stipulated under Article 3* of this Proclamation is punishable with *rigorous imprisonment from 10 to 20 years.*

Reading the text of the provision, it is hardly possible to clearly establish the three elements of the crime. First, the legal element of the offence is missing as it relies on somewhat absurdly and whole-scathingly formulated definition of a terrorist act provided under Article 3 – a definition largely contemplated as incompatible to the international laws relating to terrorism, and at odds to the international human rights standards – and hence, lacking the legality element of the crime. Second, the provision requires neither intention nor negligence as a requisite in establishing a criminal intent (*mens rea*) against the person. Third, the material element of the crime (*the actus reus*) is ironically linked to the publication vis-à-vis the likelihood of perceiving its content as an encouragement or incitement to terrorism, as there is no need to establish the actual cause and effect relationship between the publication and the allegedly targeted group to be encouraged and their actual understanding of the substance. More disturbing is the very subjective threshold *some members* of the public – a criterion which may also be satisfied even with a minimum group of two or more people – and their mere potential understanding, not their actual understanding. Then comes the penalty that extends up to twenty years rigorous imprisonment. With these criteria, not a single publication that contains views critical of the government may escape criminal liability pursuant to this provision.

88. Since the coming into force of the proclamation in 2009, cases involving dozens of journalists, bloggers, opposition political figures, and activists have been prosecuted and convicted in particular reference to Article 6 of the proclamation. Indeed, in the first anti-terrorism case – *Elias Kifle et al the Federal Public Prosecutor* – three of the five defendants were in fact journalists. In another case initiated on the same day, i.e., *Abdi Wolie Mohammed et al v. Federal Public Prosecutor*, two of the four defendants were again journalists.

89. In another prominent case, *Andualem Aragie et al v. Federal Public Prosecutor*, twenty-four politicians, journalists and activists were also charged and convicted on account of the various provisions of the Anti-Terrorism Proclamation, including that of Article 6. Nearly half of the defendants in the case were journalists, and among them is veteran journalist Eskinder Nega – whose detention was held arbitrary by the UN Human Rights Council Working Group on Arbitrary detention – sentenced to eighteen years' imprisonment.

90. There are currently dozens of pending terrorism cases, the majority of which are not in fact related to the materialised principal crimes of terrorism.[26] Instead, they are charges for the expression of ideas and participation in matters of public interest as a concerned citizen, journalist, politician or activist. Whenever the government thinks that individuals or groups are critical of its actions and policies, it uses terrorism charges to silence these dissent voices. In these charges, of course, the government uses the fight against terrorism narratives such as the participation of these individuals and groups in acts of terrorism or in encouraging and inciting others to participate in terrorism activities to destruct or destroy the Ethiopian constitutional order. In light of this, the anti-terrorism proclamation and its repercussion in thwarting the practical enjoyment of the right remains one of the most disgruntling perplexities in the present politico-legal landscape of the country.

---

26. For further follow-up of the closed and pending terrorism related cases, *see* Ethio Trial Tracker, htt ps://ethiotrialtracker.org/category/charges-in-pdf/ (accessed 4 Jan. 2018).

91. As a supplement to Article 6 of the Anti-Terrorism Proclamation, the lately adopted Proclamation on Telecom Fraud Offences (Proclamation No. 961/2012) also criminalises the use or causes the use of any telecommunications network or apparatus to disseminate any terrorising message connected with a crime punishable under the Anti-Terrorism Proclamation, as an offence punishable up to eight years' rigorous imprisonment and with a fine up to 80,000 (Eighty-Thousand) Ethiopian Birr.

92. Apart from the afore-highlighted core legislation of the country, other dispersedly stipulated limitation clauses in different proclamations, and their inevitable impact in dictating the practical essence of the right have also a paramount significance in framing the domestic normative discourse on the subject. Some of the legislation in this context are briefly noted hereunder.

V. The Proclamation on the Electoral Code of Conduct for Political Parties

93. Chief among these legislations is the Proclamation on the Electoral Code of Conduct for Political Parties. Speaking in hortatory terms, and in light of its aim which is meant to regulate the conduct of political actors in their exercise of the thickest notion of free speech and expression as a standard margin expected in the political landscape, it can be submitted that almost the entire content of the Proclamation has a direct or indirect – both positively and negatively – impact in shaping the practical value of the right and its scope of application. Duly noting this overall significance, a careful reading of the some of the specific provisions of the proclamation would further accentuate the need to assess the imitable status of the limitation clauses inserted in the proclamation.

94. To start with the positives, Article 8 of the Proclamation demands the respect for every campaigner's freedom to disseminate variegated political views, strategies, policies and programmes without any threat or intrusion. Also under Article 17, similar rights of candidates including to: freely express their political views and opinions; to publish and distribute their election materials; to display banners and billboards; and to challenge and debate the political views and opinions of others are also indisputable elements of the person's freedom of speech and expression in particular and as features of citizen's right to actively participate in the political affairs of the country.

95. More specific to the subject at hand, the Proclamation imposes the duty to respect for the freedom of the mass media. Most importantly, it prescribes any act of harassing or obstructing private or government journalists who are engaged in their professional activities during the course of any campaign.

96. Coming to the limitation clauses in the exercise of the freedom of opinion and speech, Article 11 of the Proclamation is grafted and articulated with a content that appears rather too scrappy and repugnant in light of the expected thickest margin of tolerance that must be applicable while limiting the exercise of the right in the context of the political freedom of opinion and expression. In this aspect, the Proclamation, for example, has imposed the very subjectivity-prone obligation on a Speaker at political rallies to restrain from using a language that is deemed as making inflammatory or defamatory statements. It also prescribes the issuance or distribution of pamphlets, newsletters, or posters containing language or material that threatens or incites violence.

97. Article 13 of the Proclamation also poses a similar practical challenge with its 'whole-catching' enunciation of activities under the broader notion of campaigns inciting violence or threats for violence, acts of vandalism, or public disorder committed or threatened by officials, candidates, members of supporters. In a similar vibe, Article 29 of the Proclamation also prescribes an act of disseminating information that destabilises peace and security during the election process, either by making a speech or by distributing written materials containing language that threatens to or incites for violence.

98. Then come the consequences – if an act is deemed as a violation of these restrictions – in twofold jurisdictional setups. One aspect of the measure is an administrative decision which is to be rendered either by the Joint Council (established pursuant to Article 20 of the Proclamation) or by the National Election Board. The measures range from the simpler action of giving public warning to the political party or person who is adjudged to have committed the prohibited act to that of the serious measure of cancelling the candidacy of the person or suspend the political party from running for election depending on the gravity of the act.

99. Stipulated under Article 35 of the Proclamation, the most impending measure is, however, the criminal liability to be taken by Courts against the suspect for up to three years of simple imprisonment. Such a measure can be taken by the Court, for example, against a person who is adjudged to have disseminated false information that stirs hatred or fear; or unduly influence the process or result with intent to disrupt or prevent the election process from running; or with intent to unduly influence the process or outcome of the election.

100. While outlawing calls or campaigns for violence may not be problematic in and of itself, the very subjective nature of the terms makes the limitation clauses as normative pretexts in legitimising unnecessary, disproportionate and abusive hands of the government in its uncharted power of enforcement. As evidently observed in the last five elections conducted in the country and the subsequent discomfitures, the absence of a standard precision as to what constitutes inflammatory speech, defamatory speech, or a material that threatens or incites violence has been serving to normalise the regime's repressive actions undertaken under the normative excuses of these normative limitation clauses.

101. Given that there are no exceptional and tolerable circumstances provided in the Proclamation, the discretion and the thresholds in determining whether a certain speech or expression falls under these provisions rests in the hands of the authorities in power. In the country where the political landscape is solely preserved to de facto single party monopoly under EPRDF, and where the judiciary is institutionally impotent to confront arbitrary actions of the regime in power, the inevitable and inexcusable impact of these restrictive provisions in denting the better enforcement of the right cannot be neglected as mere rhetoric.

VI. The Broadcasting Service Proclamation: Limitations on Freedom of Expression and Imparting Information

102. The other legislation that contains limitation clauses with freedom of expression and dissemination of information is the Broadcasting Service Proclamation No. 533/2008. Aimed at regulating the electronic broadcasting media, Articles 30 and 31 of the proclamation provide the list of prohibited programmes with contents that should not be disseminated by any broadcasting service.

103. Whereas the restriction imposed under Article 31 of the Proclamation on broadcasting certain programmes on the ground of protecting the well-being of children appears to have an indisputable constitutional backup, the prohibitions solicited under Article 30 are rather dubiously articulated inviting for a potential abuse in their practical application. Apart from the standard that requires any programme to reflect different and balanced viewpoints, as stipulated in paragraph 1– which is indeed the ultimate essence of the right itself – the other thresholds are far from clarity. Paragraph 2, for instance, demands to ascertain the accuracy of the content and source of the information to be transmitted. Despite the generally expected due diligence from broadcasters and journalists, such a stringent expectation tends to provoke self-censorship by shifting the unrealistically attainable burden of proving the exactitude of the information as a requisite. Similarly, every news shall also be impartial, accurate and balanced.

104. On the other hand, any programme intended to be transmitted which violates the dignity and personal liberty of mankind or the rules of good behaviour or undermine the belief of other is casted-off as illegal. Alongside, programmes that are deemed as criminal offences against the security of the State, against the constitutionally established government administration, and/or against the defence force of the country are also outlawed. Dissemination of messages alluded to maliciously accuse or defame individuals, nation/nationalities, peoples, or organisations are also included among the prohibited lists of programmes. Other messages with contents likely to cause dissension among nationalities or instigate dissension among peoples as well as programmes inciting for war are all prescribed by the proclamation. In addition, impermissible contents of advertisements are regulated in the subsequent Articles 33–36 of the proclamation.

105. Once the broadcasting service is pronounced to have violated either of these prohibitions, without prejudice to other severe penalties in pursuance to the relevant provisions of the criminal law, the Proclamation has stipulated the measures to be taken as punishment. Accordingly, while Article 45 provides a range of financial punishments in the form of fines to be paid in money, Article 46 on the other hand orders the confiscation of the property used for broadcasting, as an additional measure to the principal penalty.

106. Generally, while these grounds for restrictions may not be problematic per se, the very subjective and ambiguous nature of the thresholds would pose a greater risk of abusing these limitation clauses in denting the legitimate exercise of broadcasting and dissemination of information. The bigger disconcertment is, therefore, not the hypothetically asserted ban of these programmes. Rather it is the practical task of filtering what maximum threshold should a certain broadcasting programme manifest in order for it to constitute as an act aiming to achieve one of the above-prohibited purposes. What content of a programme is, for example, a crime against the security of the State? What kind of speech or broadcasting crimes could be committed against the government vis-à-vis the most irreplaceable role of the media in maintaining the desperately needed public scrutiny of state functioning, which in essence upholds transparent, accountable and responsible government in a democratic society? In light of these and related questions of uncertainties, if the prohibitions are to have a genuine practical meaning only to the extent of limiting some illegitimate exercising of the freedom to seek, receive, and impart information through broadcasting programmes, cementing a competent, impartial, independent, and neutral judiciary with a strong institutional courtesy to monitor and challenge government actions – usually justified through these limitations clauses – should come at the forefront.

VII. The Advertisement Proclamation and Contents Prohibited for Advertisement

107. Largely substantiated by similar grounds discussed so far, the Advertisement Proclamation No. 759/2012 also contains provisions that prohibit the production and dissemination of certain contents in the form of advertisement through any of the mass media outlets in both the print and broadcasting services. Article 6 of the Proclamation particularly describes the required content-based standards and manner of presenting advertisements. Content-wise, the advertisement should not be contrary to the law or moral; it should not be misleading; it must not be narrated with unfair statements. Advertisements are also required to respect the social and traditional values of the society and shall not infringe on the legitimate interests of consumers. Furthermore, it must describe the true nature, use, quality, and other similar information about the product or service intended to be promoted. It should also uphold the dignity and interests of the country. While these and related standards are constitutionally justified as safeguards to societal or public interest against abuse of freedom of expression, and in the context of their vital role so as to maintain a healthy competition in the free market of ideas, the restrictions stipulated under Article 7, however, are polemically speaking far from clarity in their application.

108. Article 7 proscribes unlawful or immoral advertisements with a listing of contents that are deemed to have fallen under the scope of the prohibition. Within this category are (i) advertisements that contain image, speech or comparisons that violates the dignity, liberty or equality of mankind in relation to language, gender, race, nation, nationality, profession, religion, belief, political or social status; (ii) adverts that violate rules of good behaviour or human dignity of individuals, nation, nationalities, or peoples, and defames the reputation of an organisation; (iii) messages that undermine the national or regional state's flag, emblem, national anthem or currency; (iv) content that undermines the dignity or emotional feeling of physically disabled person or HIV/AIDS or suffering from other diseases; (v) advertisement that instigate chaos, violence, terror, conflict, or fear among people, and also message that instigate an action that could endanger the physical or mental health and security of the people.

109. In addition, whereas Articles 8 and 10 of the Proclamation also proscribe misleading or unfair advertisements and adverts affecting minors respectively, on the other, Article 9 supplemented by Articles 11 and the following provisions govern the conditions, the manner and presentations of a certain type of advertisements. In a more proscriptive sense, Articles 25 and 26 of the Proclamation provide the list of totally prohibited and partially restricted advertisements. Very contestable among the list in this category is the absolute prohibition of advertisement having political goals as provided under Article 25(1(j)) of the proclamation. Regardless of some exceptions to this rule as stated under paragraph 2 of Article 25, prohibiting advertisements having, at least 'lawful' political goals would complement neither to the constitutional nor to the international human rights standards in setting the limitation on the right to freedom of expression.

110. Finally, if one is found to be in violation of these restrictions in his/her advertising activity, the consequential penalties are stipulated under Article 34 of the Proclamation: indeed, maintaining the possibility for sever penalty if any, under other relevant laws of the country.

VIII. The Computer Crime Proclamation and Limitations to Freedom of Expression

111. Perhaps the most recent legislation relevant to the subject, the Computer Crime Proclamation No. 958/2016 incorporates regulatory provisions which are reckoned to have a grave impact on the enjoyment of the right to freedom of expression online. The particular inventions of the Proclamation in the context of restraining the freedom of expression could be summarised into three perspectives: contents of data proscribed as obscene or indecent against minors; the more extended version of 'criminal' defamation; and the crimes relating to the online 'incitement of fear and violence' in the framework of national security.

112. Article 12 of the Proclamation criminalises the intentional production, transmission, sale, distribution, making available, or possession without authorisation of any picture, poster, video or image through a computer system that depicts a minor or a person appearing to be a minor in an explicit sexual conduct. On similar grounds of protecting a minor, this same provision also proscribes any act of enticing or soliciting a minor for explicit sexual conduct by transmitting or sending erotic speeches, pictures, text messages, or videos through a computer system. With no gainsaying as to the justifiability of castigating these online conducts, the provision remains, however, incomplete as it lacks a definition of the acts proscribed, such as what constitutes an act of 'erotic', 'enticing' or 'soliciting'.

113. Again on the horizontal aspect of protecting others from some abusive exercising of freedom of expression, Article 13 penalises any act of intimidating or threatening another person or his/her family with serious danger or injury by disseminating any writing, video, audio or any other image through computer systems. Furthermore, paragraph 2 prohibits the use of computer systems or keeping the victim's computer communication under surveillance in order to cause fear, threat of psychological strain on another person by sending or repeatedly transmitting information about him/her or his/her families. Then comes paragraph 3 with the crime of defamation outlawing the dissemination of any writing, video, audio or any other image through a computer system that is defamatory to the honour or reputation of another person. Article 13 seems to be redundant given that these similar conducts are already proscribed in general Criminal Code as discussed in the foregoing section. The only exception could be that the Proclamation's scope of application makes it more specific and fitting to the nature of these offences when they are committed through a computer system.

114. More controversial in its application, and arguably a provision that poses grave concerns to the better enjoyment of online freedom of expression is Article 14 of the Proclamation which invokes the more volatile conception of public security as a justification in criminalising certain online-based conducts. Notwithstanding that similar acts are punishable pursuant to Article 257 of the general Criminal Code, Article 14 echoes the illegality of intentionally disseminating through a computer system, of any written, video, audio or any other picture that incites violence, chaos, or conflict among people as punishable.

115. As criminal liability upon conviction, each of the afore-highlighted provisions of the Proclamation has stipulated the corresponding penalties in the form of either simple or rigorous imprisonment and/or fines. While the maximum sentence in the form of physical confinement is imposed upon conviction of the crimes stipulated under Articles 12 and 13(2) of the Proclamation, which may result in up to ten years rigorous imprisonment, and the highest monetary penalty is a fine up to 50,000 Ethiopian Birr when a person is found guilty of disseminating advertisement messages through email or other computer addresses without obtaining prior consent from the recipient with the intent to advertise or sell any product or service as enshrined under Article 13 of the Proclamation.

116. Generally, what could be asserted from the discussion so far is the fact that – notwithstanding the incomplete, scattered and sketchy features of the national statutory regulatory framework – the constitutional and the fundamental right to freedom of opinion and expression is one of the most practically scrutinised and routinely constricted right in the country.

117. Apart from these legislative-based regulatory schemes on the limits to the enjoyment of the right, the pivotal role of non-legal monitoring mechanisms of controlling and preventing dissemination of certain ideas are also the de facto integral components of the freedom of expression and media landscape administration outfit. In this regard, the informal monitoring settings through technical measures of surveillance, filtering and blocking; the policy-backed monopolistic government ownership, provision, and administration of the media and Internet outlets; the fright-based self-censorship; and the massive recruitment of actors tasked with the spreading and vending of pro-government contents in the social media have been serving as the most indelible apparatuses in shaping the substantial, institutional, and procedural facets of the right.[27]

27. Albeit its narrowly formulated scope only in the context of the Internet regulatory frameworks in Ethiopia, *see also* Halefom H. Abraha, *Examining Approaches to Internet Regulation in Ethiopia*, Inform. Commun. Technol. Law, DOI: 10.1080/13600834.2017.1374057 (2017), 309–311.

Part II. Regulation of Print Media

118. Perhaps the oldest modality in the modern media history of the country, the print media outlet is thought to have been introduced in Ethiopia as early as in 1900s with the then first hand-written publication of *Aemiro* (brain) *Gazette* in 1902. Quite contrary to such a long-standing history, however, the print media has never been a powerful and well-expanded means of disseminating ideas and information. While there are multiple reasons for this, the authoritarian and oppressive nature of the Ethiopian government is the main contributing factor. The government perceives the freedom of expression exercised through the print media as a challenge to its monopoly of information and public debate. Moreover, illiteracy and the rural nature of the Ethiopian society are other impediments to the flourishment of the print media. Even the literacy rate in Ethiopia is still close to half its total population (49.1%).[28] Furthermore, the circulation of the handful of printed press is known for its irregularity. It is also inaccessible as the distribution does not reach beyond the capital, Addis Ababa, and in the few other big cities of the country, thus targeting only the urban elite. The linguistic coverage of the newspapers and magazines is another hurdle as 90% of the print media are published only in Amharic and English.[29]

119. Up until the early 1990s only a few state-owned magazines had been operational. In fact, with due cognisance to the then promising development of the independent media through different publications during the historically imprinted student movements in 1960s. It was only in the immediate aftermath of the reign of the Transitional Government that the country witnessed a massive proliferation of private newspapers and magazines. Booming at the peak level for a short period during the most democratically contested third electoral campaign in the year 2005, to the regret of many, such a mushrooming evolvement immediately started to gigantically clamped down following the subsequent post-2005 national election political dismays rewritten in the country.[30]

---

28. *See* the CIA World Factbook, https://www.cia.gov/library/publications/the-world-factbook/fields/2103.html (accessed 7 Jan. 2018).
29. FOJO: Media Institute, Lineaus University & Swedish Embassy Ethiopia, *Feasibility Study: Strengthening Free, Independent, and Professional Journalism in Ethiopia,* https://fojo.se/images/documents/Etiopien/Fojo-Feasibilitity-Study-Media-Ethiopia_final.pdf (accessed 10 Jan. 2018).
30. On the historical aspect of media in Ethiopia, *see* Reta Meseret, *The Quest for Press Freedom: One Hundred Years of History of the Media in Ethiopia* (University Press of America 2013).

120. Unsurprisingly, therefore, the print media regulatory framework of the country remains incomplete as it is short of providing full-fledged and comprehensive normative standards and principles governing the proper administration of the press and actors involved in the business. For that matter, there is no separate legislation that is exclusively destined to regulate the print media. Hence, while addressing the various issues pertaining to this category of mass media, one has to make an inquiry to the proclamations of the country with the more general scope of application; the most germane of which being Freedom of the Mass Media and Access to Information Proclamation No. 590/2008.

Chapter 1. The Journalists' Profession

121. Before rummaging into the details as to the conditions and requirements to get involved in a journalistic work, and the corresponding guarantees and duties therein, noting the nitty-gritty as to difference between the conception of a journalist as an individual professional and the exercising of journalistic activity by establishing a certain print media outlet in whatsoever format – such as periodical, newspaper, magazine, or satire – would serve as a basis to better analyse the legal requisites to practice journalism in Ethiopia. Accordingly, the first query relates to the main subject of this part of the monograph which starts by highlighting the question of what kind of mass media constitutes a print media outlet? The second question to arise is the issue of who is a journalist, and who can engage in journalistic work as an individual person in Ethiopia? Then comes the issue of who can own or establish a print mass media, and under what conditions and/or, which procedural and formality requirements are supposed to be fulfilled? In the sections to follow, an attempt is made to address these and related issues.

§1. The Print Media

122. As one of the most conventionally known mass media outlets, the print media is usually perceived as the typical means of exercising freedom of speech through printed matter including that of periodicals. The Freedom of Expression and Access to Information Proclamation No. 590/2008 (hereinafter the Press Proclamation) defines the phrase 'printed matter' under Article 2(2), as a whole-inclusive term implying the non-exhaustive list of all materials:

> … intended for public distribution including mass media but also other printed material–including musical works, plays, pictures, cartoons, books, pamphlets, posters and commercial advertisings as well as audio, visual and audio-visual recordings, motion pictures and the likes.

Such a general definitional approach, nonetheless, does not include materials such as official printed matters, notices, minutes, reports, and decisions of legislative, judicial or executive organs. Other materials only intended for the purpose of commerce and transport, domestic and social life, such as forms, price lists, printed advertising matter, family advertisements, postcards, pictorial reproductions, annual business and administrative reports, as well as election documents are also beyond the scope of the definition.

123. The emblematic modality of the print media, i.e., a periodical, is on the other hand defined under Article 2(3) of the Press Proclamation as: 'a printed material which is scheduled to appear in regular sequences of at least twice a year, which has a fixed title and which has a general distribution aimed at the entire public or a section thereof, and includes newspapers and magazines'. Accordingly, for a certain material to constitute a periodical, the conditions of maintaining its consistency and regular sequence within a certain time interval; its distinctive name or title; and its reachability at least to a certain section of the society are set as defining features of a periodical which includes newspapers and magazines.

§2. A Journalist as a Professional

124. None of the relevant federal proclamations provides a normative definitional and functional scope of a 'journalistic' profession. Intriguingly though, such a definition is stipulated under the City of Addis Ababa Mass Media Agency Establishment Proclamation No. 20/2009. Article 2(2) of this Proclamation provides a more inclusive approach outlining a journalist as an 'employee who is engaged in reporting, editing, producing, painting, photography, taking video and organising the same, directing film, working as technician of production or generally engaged in different reports that are to be broadcasted to the public'.[31] Apart from such a task or role-based-approach in describing the term, no specific educational expertise is required as a condition in order to pursue a journalism profession as a career; certainly not a certificate from a journalism school is a must to have. Tellingly, the very recent history of the professional journalism education itself – which was in fact inaugurated on a permanent basis in 1996 following the establishment of the former Ethiopian Mass Media Training Institute that was then merged with the present undergraduate School of Journalism and Communication of Addis Ababa University – would explicate the status of professional journalism – *sensu stricto* – in Ethiopia. This said, promisingly, the very recent composition of employing press has seen an increasing number of journalists with specialised degrees in journalism and/or communication, and at least, the absolute majority of them have completed a university degree, though not necessarily in journalism. One may contend, therefore, that even if a certain statutorily stipulated qualification has not been set as a requisite to engage in a journalistic activity, there seems to have an encouraging trend of practicing journalism by those certified as journalists by profession.

125. Coming to the normative entitlement of working as a journalist in Ethiopia, the scope of the protection to the right appears to be entangled with the requisite of possessing Ethiopian nationality. As clearly stipulated under Article 5 of the Press Proclamation, only Ethiopians have the right to work in or establish a mass media. If a foreign journalist intends to enter into the country with his/her journalistic mission – be it for a particular event coverage or for a relatively unlimited journalistic role – he/she must first apply and obtain a journalist visa. Such a procedure is mostly undertaken at the respective embassies and consular offices of Ethiopia. More stringently, the application for such a special visa requires submission of detail information, such as a kit-list of the tools the journalist intends to take with and other relevant supporting documents authenticating his/her task.

31. Addis Ababa City Administration Council, *A Proclamation to Establish the Mass Media Agency of Addis Ababa City Government*, Proclamation No. 20/2009, Addis Negari Gazeta, 1st year, No. 20 (Addis Ababa, 2009).

126. The impact of this nationality-based restriction on the right to practice a journalistic profession is of a twofold. For one thing, it undermines the 'whole-inclusive' character of the right to freedom of opinion and expression that is constitutionally granted to 'everyone' as subjects of the right. Second, in light of the fact that the Ethiopian nationality law does not recognise dual-citizenship, the Ethiopian diaspora who hold state's passport are also virtually excluded. This makes the purpose and objective of the restriction more precarious and to the detriment of Ethiopians who should have been for all the possible reasons entitled to take part in the free market of ideas in all aspects of Ethiopian affairs.

§3. The Status of Bloggers: Full Journalists?

127. Thanks to the pioneering global Internet transformation, the ever-growing influence of online blogging either in the form of an online journal or through a website has also become a common activity of fringe journalism, writing, publishing and disseminating ideas of various kind in the very Ethiopian media landscape. In fact, given that the government-owned *Ethio-Telecom* is the sole provider of Internet services, and as a country with one of the lowest Internet penetration rates in the world estimated only 4.3%,[32] the impact of blogging and Internet-based mass media in general remains at an infant level.

128. It is therefore unsurprising that none of the recently proclaimed laws of the country has this new platform got attention. Even the most pertinent legislation on the subject, i.e., the Proclamation on Telecom Fraud Offences (761/2012) and the Computer Crimes Proclamations (958/2016) have made no normative standings in particular reference to the work of blogging or bloggers. Indeed, as discussed hitherto regarding the general restrictions of freedom of opinion and expression, these proclamations have contained both prohibitive and punitive provisions as regulatory frameworks monitoring the exercise of the right through computer and telecommunication services (which also includes Internet). Apart from these general restrictive measures and the penal consequences thereof, in nowhere is the particular legal status of bloggers exclusively governed.

129. The practical usage of the term does not help either, in clarifying the context in which the work of blogging is being comprehended. It is not uncommon to use interchangeably of terms such as journalist, blogger, human rights activist or advocate, analyst or expert. At times, as evidently noticeable in practice, there is no gainsaying that a journalist by profession could be very active in the online mass media through his/her publications aiming for human rights activism or advocacy so that it would not be problematic of naming the person with any of the terms. As noted earlier, even the more conventionally known profession 'journalist' itself is not clearly defined with certain distinguishing features in the relevant laws.

---

32. *See* the Internet World Stats Usage and Population Statistics: The Internet Coaching Library, http://www.internetworldstats.com/africa.htm#et (accessed 13 Feb. 2018).

130. This being the case, however, simply equating the work of 'journalism' with that of 'blogging' or synonymising a 'journalist' with a 'blogger' would invite more challenges than the pursuit of a wider protection to the online exercising of freedom of expression through blogging. For instance, as it stands, no requirement of official registration and licensing of a blog platform is a condition for a blogger whereas a journalist is duty bound to officially register and secure the required license in order to engage in the print mass media through periodicals. These requisites, alongside many other procedural and formality requirements, would make the traditionally known practice of journalism through periodicals more precarious than the functionally easily operated work of blogging. Accordingly, in light of at least the procedural and substantial requirements to practice journalist activities, it can be argued that a work of journalism can be done through blogging but not every blogging work may constitute journalistic activity. Similarly, every journalist maybe at the same time be considered as a blogger depending on the online platform he/she operates but not every blogger could be treated as a journalist. Such differences in the nature of the role, and the conditions and the elements to be fulfilled for a professional journalist work, arguably would portray that not all bloggers could be contemplated as full journalists in the strict sense of the term; least in the Ethiopian context.

131. In connection to the work of blogging in Ethiopia and its regulatory framework, the famous case of the group called *Zone 9* bloggers deserve a special mention. A group of ten bloggers started their online blogging in around May 2012 focusing in their writings on various issues that the country has been facing under the current regime: cases of human rights violations, rule of law, constitutionalism, good governance, education, non-violent social transformation, corruption, and many other problems to mention few. In terms of their professional composition, they are comprised of journalists, lawyer, engineer, economist, IT expert, data expert, writer, and university lecturer.

132. Following their influential achievements in revolutionising the online social media as a suitable platform, attracting the youth for dialogues on different debatable and disquieting concerns of public interest, the Ethiopian government had arrested and detained six of the bloggers along with three independent journalists in April 2014 alleging that their conduct constituted incitement of chaos and violence through online website and an outrage to the constitution and the constitutional order.

133. After a period of about four months of pre-charge detention, on 17 July 2014, they were formally charged with a rather unspecific crime of terrorism in accordance with general inference to Article 4 of the Anti-Terrorism Proclamation No. 652/2009.[33] As the hearing proceeded, despite the Court's order to amend the charge demanding clarity regarding the specific terrorist act that the defendants were

33. *See* the details about the Charge: Ministry of Justice Federal Prosecutor File No. 05/07 & Federal Police Investigation File No. 601/06 (08/11/2006 E.C.). [copy of the file with the authors].

alleged to have committed, the same terrorism charge was replicated linking the group to one of the proscribed militant opposition force called *Ginbot* 7.[34]

134. Almost after a year and a half detention period pending trial, the Prosecutor dropped the charge against the five of the bloggers in July 2015, in what was interpreted by many as a pretentious show and image building stratagem in preparation to host the then US President Barack Obama's visit to Ethiopia. Soon after, the charge against the other four of the bloggers was dismissed, resulting in their acquittal from jail in October 2015. The hearing over the case, however, continued at the appellate Federal Supreme Court following the prosecutor's appeal against the acquittal of the four bloggers by the Federal High Court. In its verdict rendered on the 6th of April 2017, while upholding the lower court's acquittal of the two bloggers, the Supreme Court disagreed with the lower court on the acquittal of the other two adjudging that even if their conducts did not constitute as terrorist crimes, the defendants should defend an ordinary criminal charge of 'provocation and incitement for violence by word of mouth, disseminating images or writings proscribed under Article 257(a & e) of the general Revised Criminal Code.

135. Leaving aside the myriad of issues pertaining to the merits of the accusations having been instituted against the bloggers, what is not disputable is the fact that Ethiopia has not yet adopted any separate legislation that regulates exclusively of the blogging media platform or the work of bloggers. As evident from all the criminal cases brought against bloggers, the pertinent provisions of the general Criminal Code, the Anti-Terrorism Proclamation and other relevant laws have been invoked as the normative basis. [35] What is being monitored in accordance with the extant laws that the country has adopted so far is, therefore, not blogging as one of the media outlet – like broadcasting or periodicals – rather it is the content-based scrutiny against the speech of the individual person regardless of his/her status as a blogger.

§4. Ownership and Running Print Mass Media

136. As stated under Article 5 of the Press Proclamation, every Ethiopian national has the right to establish a mass media outlet including that of a periodical, be it in the form of newspapers or magazines. This being the principle, there are certain exceptions that are deemed to justify restrictions to ownership of the media outlet. Apart from the unequivocal exclusion of non-Ethiopians not to engage in this sector, Article 7 paragraph 6 of the Proclamation bestows the right to own and run mass media – broadcasting, periodical or new agency – only to juridical person, and hence an individual human person cannot engage in these activities on his/her own

34. Ministry of Justice Federal Prosecutor File No. 05/07 & Federal Police Investigation File No. 08/06 (Date:06/05/2007 E.C). [Copy of the file with the authors].

35. For further details regarding the other cases brought against members of the zone 9 bloggers and many other independent journalists, *see* https://www.ethiotrialtracker.org/latest-vital-information-on-ethiopians-charged-with-terrorism/ (accessed 14 Feb. 2018).

personal capacity. Hence, a joint reading of both provisions would indicate that operating a printed mass media entails the establishment of a company either the total capital of which originates from a local source, or its capital and voting rights are held by Ethiopian nationals. Even a company whose capital or voting rights are held by locally registered business organisations in which foreign nationals have voting rights in its internal functioning cannot engage in this business. On the other hand, associations – as long as they are registered as a local association in accordance with the charities and association law – may be involved in the printed mass media.

137. Furthermore, notwithstanding the fulfilment of the nationality requisite, Article 7 of the Press Proclamation has also narrated additional circumstances under which the right to engage in mass media activities may be expelled.

138. The first prohibition relates to ownership of multiple print mass media at the same time. In this regard, one of the relevant governing rules under Article 7(2) of the Press Proclamation ejects that:

> Any person who exercises direct or indirect effective control over a company holding a nation-wide license or a license for an area with a recorded population of more than 100,000 inhabitants may not exercise direct or indirect effective control over a company operating a periodical servicing the same or an overlapping market.

A methodical reading of the provision would reveal three cumulative elements to be established for its application: first, it must be ascertained that the person has a direct or indirect effective control of an already existing broadcasting company; second, it must be established that the said company holds either a nation-wide broadcasting license or a license to broadcast within an area whereby more than 100,000 inhabitants are recorded; and third, it needs to be proven that the new periodical is intended to serve the same or an overlapping market.

139. As an extension to this restriction over ownership of a periodical on the afore-stated grounds, paragraph 3 of Article 7 inserts further criteria as conditions to restrain a person's pursuit of owning a periodical. Accordingly, once the person has a direct or indirect effective control over a company that operates a periodical published a given language, this same person may not exercise the same right of effectively controlling another periodical published in the same language that is servicing the same or an overlapping market. In contrast, while paragraph 2 of Article 7 prohibits effective control of two or more companies running broadcasting and periodicals at the same time in the circumstances specified therein, paragraph 3 on the other forbids the right to exercise effective control over two companies operating periodicals published in the same language and within the same market.

140. Setting aside the debate as to the legitimacy of restricting ownership of a periodical merely on the stated grounds – the purpose and objective of which is far from clear – more perplexing is the lack of lucidity of the terms that formulate the extent of the prohibition in both paragraphs. The key phrase 'direct or indirect effective control' as a threshold for the prohibition could be quoted as a typical example of such an ambiguity. Of course, conceding this obscurity, which risks the practical efficacy of the restriction in a fiddle-footed status, paragraph 4 of Article 7 has demanded the promulgation of a special law that would set the procedures in determining and assessing the threshold of 'effective control' as it stands in the provision. To the knowledge of this author, a legislation to this effect is yet to be adopted. Accordingly, the transitory standard as enshrined under the same paragraph 4, which assumes 'holding at least fifteen percent of the share or the capital of the company in question' as a satisfying factual indication of direct or indirect control of the person over the company would stand as the defining element while assessing the criterion. Even with this benchmark, other issues including, for instance, what constitutes an overlapping market area, and under what yardsticks such a boundary is to be drawn, are not aptly addressed.

141. Not only on the controversial issue of who can own and run the print mass media in Ethiopia, the Press Proclamation has also been subject to critics in particular reference to the stringent procedural requirements for registration of any periodical to be published and distributed in Ethiopia. Article 9 of the proclamation demands anyone who desires to publish a periodical to apply for its registration by providing the required information in pursuance to paragraph 3 of the provision.

142. Before digging into the necessitated particulars for registration, it seems logically appealing to identify the competent authority entrusted to issue the certificate of registration. Literal inference to Article 9 paragraph 1 of the Press Proclamation will be misleading given that the former Ministry of Information and the regional information bureaus – which were mandated to effect the registration at the federal and regional level respectively – have ceased to exist, and are replaced by the Federal Government Communication Affairs Office and State's Government Communication Affairs Offices for each regional state members of the federation. The Federal Government Communication Affairs Office was created pursuant to the Council of Ministers Regulation 158/2008.[36] Albeit the official transfer of the rights and obligations of the former Ministry of Information to that the present Government Communication Affairs Office pursuant to Article 10 of the Regulation in general terms, the specific regulatory powers of the former Ministry of Information in regards to press are, however, handed to the EBA in accordance with Article 11(2) of the Regulation. Having this shift of mandate in mind, Article 9 paragraph 1 of the Press Proclamation is thus amended by Article 11 paragraph 2 of the Council of Ministers Regulation 158/2008 in regards to the competent authority in charge of registering periodicals.

143. Accordingly, a periodical which is intended to be distributed in more than one regional state will have to be registered and licensed by the EBA. On the other hand, where the distribution of the proposed periodical is restricted only within the

---

36. FDRE Council of Ministers, *Government Communication Affairs Office Establishment Regulation No. 158/2008*, Federal Negarit Gazeta, 15th year No. 13 (Addis Ababa, 1 Jan. 2009).

territory of a single Regional State, the concerned Regional Government Communication Bureau will assume the power of registration.

144. As stipulated under Article 9(2) of the Press Proclamation, application for registration demands submission of almost every detail about the proposed periodical. This makes the registration process highly bureaucratic and perturbing. Delving into the mandatory particulars to be submitted for registration, the applicant has to first specify the name and address of the publisher or any branch offices if any. Then the name of the projected periodical needs to be indicated. Mentioning the proposed name allows the Authority to verify whether there exists an already registered periodical with a name or emblem that tends to be similar so that a potential confusion between the two periodicals could be rectified in advance, either by altering or by completely changing the name of the newly proposed periodical.

145. In addition, the name(s) and address(s) of the person(s) who hold more than 2% of the shares of the publishing company alongside the specific amount of their respective share must also be provided. The significance of providing this information may be concomitant to the task assessing the degree of 'direct or indirect effective control' of the company, which is presented as a threshold while monitoring the prohibition of double ownership of a mass media. As briefly noted earlier, however, at least as a transitional solution until a special law is to be adopted for this effect, holding a minimum of the 15% share of ownership of the company was marked as a yardstick pursuant to Article 7(4) of the Proclamation. The question that lacks clarity is, therefore, why and for what purpose the registration formality requires the disclosure of the names and the specific amount of the shares of those who hold as minimum as 2% (+), rather than sticking to the already affixed 15% ownership share. As it stands, the lowered requirement of naming persons holding between 2% and 15% of ownership shares of the company appears to serve no purpose other than unnecessarily hardening the procedure.

146. Once the application is submitted fulfilling all the required information, the registration becomes effectual either formally or presumptively. Registration is deemed formally acquired when the authority issues a certificate of registration. However, the Authority's failure to issue the certificate does not imply de facto rejection, hence there is no implied refusal. As clearly cemented under paragraph 5 of Article 9, rejection of the application for registration has to be always explicitly announced. Accordingly, if the Authority fails to react either by officially issuing the certificate or by announcing its decision of rejection in writing to the applicant including the grounds for the decision within one month since the date of submission of the application, the periodical is deemed officially registered.

Chapter 2. Journalists' Rights

147. As is the case with many other issues entertained so far, none of the media-related legislation of the country contains a comprehensively articulated normative provision with a full-fledged and complete list of the rights that a journalist is entitled in his/her professional capacity. Even Article 5(2) of the Press Proclamation – the sole provision which is framed particularising journalists as right holders – cements only the right to form or join into a professional association of their own choice. Narrating the various rights of journalists entails, therefore, methodical reference, interpretation, and application of the more broadly formulated protections to the general mass media and to every individual alike. Furthermore, the value of some of the provisions of the Press Proclamation that regulate the powers and functions of particular journalistic roles – such as the powers of 'editor-in-chief' – in maintaining the utmost possible safeguards to journalistic works should also be duly consulted.

148. In this context, Article 4 of the Proclamation which restated the constitutional freedom to mass media comes at the forefront., The prohibition of censorship entitles the journalist, as the master-brain of any mass media activity, freedom from external or internal interference in the exercise of his/her journalistic activities. The freedom to seek, receive and impart information is another aspect of the right of journalists. Most importantly, the freedom to express their opinion or criticism on various issues and their privilege to participate in the process of forming public opinion are also the key guarantees that journalists are granted under paragraph 3 of Article 4, which stems from the irreplaceable value of their professional contributions to enhance the culture of productive dialogue in all matters of public interest.

149. Perhaps indispensable in outlawing de facto censorship and discriminatory treatment of journalistic works, Article 8 of the Proclamation has forbidden any content-based discrimination by distributors either in the delivery of their service or in the determination of the price. The journalists' right to have equal access to distribution service with equal fees regardless of the content of their journalistic work becomes indispensable especially if one takes note of the fact that the majority of the printing and distribution service providers are owned by the state. In this regard, there have been occasions in which the state-owned *Birhanina Selam Printing Enterprise* – the only company with the capacity to offer the printing service on regular basis in large amount – blocks the distribution of certain newspapers with contents critical of the government by either delaying or totally refusing its printing service.[37] Accordingly, strictly implementing the spirit of Article 8 would minimise these kinds of arbitrary censorships by the printing companies and their hindrances detrimental to practicing professional journalism.

37. Human Rights Watch, *Journalism is Not a Crime: Violations of Media Freedom in Ethiopia*, https://www.hrw.org/sites/default/files/reports/ethiopia0115_ForUploadR.pdf (accessed 10 Feb. 2018).

150. Having these general entitlements in mind, their role as watchdogs of the society, the status of the normative protections to their independence, and the level of the protection to journalistic sources are respectively discussed in what follows.

§1. ROLE OF JOURNALISTS AS WATCHDOGS OF SOCIETY

151. The role of the mass media and particularly of journalists as superintendents of all government-societal undertakings is arguably their most inherent professional function: a huge task level-headedly invoked as a justification in typifying their status as the fourth state. This status puts journalists in a position to aptly watchdog the daily functioning of the state and its polity, one which is essential in maintaining the utmost values of democracy. In the words of Nelson Mandela, 'a critical, independent, and investigative press is the lifeblood of any democracy'.[38]

152. Looking at many of the preamble paragraphs of the Ethiopian Press Proclamation, at least at the outset, cementing the role of journalists as genuine overseers appear to be echoed as one of the key driving forces necessitating the enactment of the law. In this context, paragraph 5 of the preamble, for example, acknowledges the indispensable role that a free, independent, and diverse mass media with high ethical standards and professional competences plays in the national endeavour to build a democratic order in Ethiopia. Similarly, its function in promoting and ensuring respect for the fundamental rights and freedoms guaranteed by the Constitution, peace, democracy, equality, and justice is also clearly reverberated in paragraph 6 of the preamble. Most pertinently, the Proclamation also reaffirms the fundamental importance of the media in consolidating the values of transparency and accountability in the conduct of public affairs by imposing an obligation on public officials facilitate access to information so that matters of public interest may be exposed, discussed and debated. This demand is further strengthened by the recognition of the right to the media to collect and disseminate information, including of a critical nature stressing that the need for an independent media that serves as a public forum for uninhibited democratic dialogue.

153. Apart from these preambular paragraphs, the Proclamation also embodies provisions aimed at ensuring journalists' watchdog function. Chief among these is Article 4 paragraph 3 of the Proclamation which imposes various obligations on public bodies in facilitating the role of the mass media in fulfilling its public function. To begin with, as the task of scrutinising state functioning is hardly attainable if accesses to all daily happenings are blocked, all the public bodies[39] are obliged to have regard to the right of the mass media to seek, receive and impart information. It is also the duty of these bodies to respect and ensure the media's right to express

38. FOJO: Media Institute et al., *supra* note 29, 6.
39. A 'Public Body' is defined under Art. 2(5) of the Press Proclamation as: 'anybody established under the Federal Constitution or State Constitution or any other law which forms part of any level or branch of the federal or regional state or owned, controlled or directly or indirectly substantially financed by funds provided by the federal or regional governments or accountable to the federal or regional states'.

opinion and criticism on various issues. Most notably, they are also obligated to and respect the media's endeavour to lead and participate in the process of forming public opinion. In a more formidable tone, paragraph 4 of Article 4 forbids any administrative measure that impairs freedom of the mass media except those restrictions enacted in accordance with limits prescribed in the constitution.

154. In a similar context, Article 11 of the Proclamation, which narrates the main objectives of ensuring the right to access to information also restates the necessity of the right, among other things, 'to foster a culture of transparency, accountability and efficiency in the functions of public bodies and to encourage and promote good governance'. Furthermore, it is indisputable that the more journalists get swift access to public information, the better they could effectively and efficiently perform their watchdog function in the society. It seems in due cognisance to this demand of urgency that Article 14(9 & 10) of the Proclamation requires the public body to respond to the requested information within a period of not more than ten working days if the applicant is a journalist whose main engagement is the dissemination of information in the mass media. What is expected in the course of demanding such a precipitate response is that the journalist reasonably demonstrates that an action taken or about to be taken by the public body should be released to the public immediately. Notwithstanding the questionability of whether a ten working days discretion itself meets the required threshold of propinquity, alongside the practical uneasiness in the implementation of even such a 'ten days' limitation period on the public bodies, at least the law's preferential treatment of journalists in fostering the efficacy of their watchdog function should not be left unnoticed. In light of these normative standards, the law's recognition of the watchdog role of journalists appears to have the required legal backup in the Ethiopian media law.

155. This said, as countless reports documented by the concerned domestic and international advocates of free speech and journalistic rights would reveal, the reality on the ground does not seem to uphold and complement the above asserted objectives of the Press Proclamation.[40] Referring to the worrying number of journalists in jail and those who remain in exile escaping persecution on grounds of their critical views against the government, Ethiopia is branded as one of the most notorious countries known for their violation of journalistic rights.

156. To this end, the much-talked-about policy of the country which advocates rather misleading narration of the doctrine of 'developmental journalism' has been notably influential in exacerbating the situation. As defined under the 2008 draft development journalism policy of Ethiopia – a document prepared and published by Ethiopian Press Agency but never nationally approved as a final policy document – developmental journalism is:

---

40. *See*, for example, Human Rights Watch, *Journalism is Not a crime': Violations of Media Freedom in Ethiopia*, http://www.hrw.org/reports/2015/01/20/journalism-not-crime (accessed 24 Jul. 2017); Committee to Protect Journalists, *CPJ Urges Ethiopia's Zenawi to Pursue Press Reforms*, http://cpj.org/2010/02, 2010 (accessed 24 Jul. 2017); Committee to Protect Journalists, *Conflating Terrorism and Journalism in Ethiopia*, https://cpj.org/2015/04/attacks-on-the-press-conflating-terrorism-and-journalism-in-ethiopia.php (accessed 24 Jul. 2017).

> a journalism that makes people understand, accept and actively participate in the implementation of appropriate development ideas that may extricate people from poverty and backwardness by bringing about rapid national change and building on positive values of development and democratic change.[41]

Legally speaking, the non-binding character of the document as it is not a proclaimed law, and even its unapproved status as an official national policy of the country may compel one to contemplate the irrelevancy of addressing the document.[42] Practically speaking, however, it is a document which is actually guiding and serving as a journalistic standard-setter in the current media landscape of the country, and hence its value cannot be underestimated. Saying this regarding its actual use, the main content of the definition and its impact in twisting the watchdog function of journalism simply into an applauder of the policies, programmes and strategies of the government in power could be observed from two perspectives. On the one hand, the definition depicts a journalist merely as a positive and success storyteller focusing on a one-sided narration that aims to invigorate economic development and rapid national change. This perception shifts the role of a journalist from that of the conventionally expected task of reporting as an outsider towards that of an active change agent who is requested to promote what is done, rather than emphasising on what should have been done and reflections on what must be done as rectifying alternatives. This approach has little or no room for critical, investigative, and research-based coverage of a certain event that is deemed sensitive to the developmental agenda of the state.[43]

157. As those operating outside this 'journalistic standard' are likely to be named and shamed as cynics and detractors of the development goals of the country, such a tendency undermines the inherent job of a journalist as a critical observer that a functioning democracy demands most. The more critical journalism is diluted, the higher the risk becomes of normalising arbitrariness, corruption, unaccountable and irresponsible governance, and most dangerously the inevitable fracture in government-public interaction. Boldly speaking, that seems where the country has been driven into, as demonstrated in largely protracted ongoing protests, civilian unrests, ethnic tensions and other multifaceted destructions that are being orchestrated since the last few years.

---

41. Ethiopian Press Agency, *Ethiopian Policy Document on Development Journalism* (2008).
42. For more details about the policy document, *see* Abayneh Mihret, *The Practice of Development Journalism in the Ethiopian Media Landscape,* LL.M Thesis, Graduate School of Journalism and Communication (Addis Ababa University 2017).
43. Terje S. Skjerdal, *Development Journalism Revived: The Case of Ethiopia*, 32 *Ecquid Novi: Afr. J. Stud.* 58–74 (2011); *See also* Terje S. Skjerdal, *The Ethiopian Journalist: Loyalist and Change Agent,* https://epub.ub.uni-muenchen.de/29707/1/Country_%20report_Ethiopia.pdf (accessed 16 Feb. 2018).

§2. JOURNALISTS' INDEPENDENCE

158. If the watchdog role of a journalist is to have any practical meaning, ensuring an independent and autonomous environment in the work journalism becomes not just an amicable luxury rather as the foundational element that defines the veracity of the profession itself. Independence permits a journalist to fully own his/her job solely guided by the law, the professional ethics, and his/her conscience as there is no room for undue influence or intervention of any kind. Independence empowers a journalist to serve the public and prioritise public interest instead of acting as a mouthpiece and passive agent for hegemonic elites untouchably comforted at the whim of the political and the economic muscles.

159. Delving into the normative safeguards to journalists' independence in the Ethiopian legal scaffold, the constitutional prohibition of any form of censorship comes at the forefront. Accordingly, as the typical manifestation of everyone's freedom of expression without any interference, the Constitution has prohibited control and supervision of the flow of information and ideas – such as probing the content of periodicals before publication– with an intent to alter, to expunge or to totally suspend their distribution. Not only is the journalists' right to practice independent journalism protected, Article 29(4) of the Constitution also demands the ensuing legal protection to the press as an institution in order for it to ensure its operational independence and its capacity to entertain diverse opinions. Furthermore, state ownership or control of the media may never be invoked as a factor in mitigating the duty of ensuring journalists' independence. Accordingly, the requirement of warranting independency and autonomy of a journalist has nothing to do with the fact of whether the journalist works in the public or the private print media. Such a 'whole-inclusive' requisite can be deduced from the constitutional provision of Article 29(5) which requires the media financed by or under the control of the State to operate in a manner that ensures the capacity of entertaining diverse opinion. Needless to say, such an objective will never be achieved if the journalist is compelled to operate in a system that impairs his/her discretion of entertaining diverse views.

160. In complement to these constitutional principles, the Press Proclamation also contains protective provisions advocating for independent journalism. While Article 4(1) of the Proclamation echoes the prohibition of censorship in any form, paragraph 4 of this same provision supplements the notion by forbidding any administrative measure that impairs the freedom of the mass media. Most crucial in maintaining journalistic independence is the unconditional autonomy accorded to the editor-in-chief. Lucidly cemented under Article 6(1):

> The mandate of the editor-in-chief designated by the publisher encompasses the power to supervise the publication of the periodical and to determine the contents thereof in such a way that nothing may be printed therein against his will. Any practice or agreement that restricts this power shall be null and void.

A careful reading of the text elucidates the three fundamental aspects of the provision that would heighten the normative protection to journalistic independence. First and for most, the discretion to supervise and determine the content of a periodical and its administration should remain as an exclusive mandate of the editor-in-chief, and hence, no other external body may intervene regardless of his/her political or whatsoever hierarchical supremacy. Second, the degree of the prohibition of such an intervention goes to the extent that nothing may be printed against the chief editors will. Third, even a wilful agreement involving the chief editor or any de facto inclination that accepts a room for intervention against this mandate is declared *null and void ab initio*, so that the chief editor cannot bargain any deal to the detriment of affecting his/her autonomy in the administration of the periodical.

161. Notwithstanding the afore-highlighted constitutional and legislative back-ups aimed at ensuring journalists' independence, the reality on the ground offers little – if not none at all – in substantiating the pragmatic observance of the law. As repetitively submitted, the repressive aspects of the law that impose severe criminal and civil liabilities on journalists, and the misleadingly advocated narration of 'developmental journalism' by the regime has exacerbated the pervasiveness of fright-based self-censorship, and the political influence and dictation of journalist work as typical features of the Ethiopian media display. Accordingly, ensuring journalists' independence has proven to be a troublesome task.

§3. Protection of Journalistic Sources

162. Protection of journalistic sources is an integral component or even the cornerstone of the press freedom. Most importantly, the watchdog role of journalism in informing the public on matters of public interest would have a meaningful outcome only if assisted by sources that may have to be maintained confidentially. Indeed, protecting the confidentiality of those who collaborated in exposing sensitive information in the public interest and ensuring their safety from the consequential risks and pressures should be asserted as the principal reflection of the journalist's ethical and professional maturity.[44]

163. Despite such an indubitable significance of preserving journalistic sources undisclosed, both for the betterment of investigative journalism, and for the protection of dedicated informants, nowhere in the Constitution or in the Press Proclamation is the right conferred a normative safeguard. Quite contrary to such a conventionally envisaged protection, Article 30(2) of the Ethiopian Broadcasting Proclamation appears to impose the burden of disclosing journalistic sources by requiring to ascertain the accuracy of the content and its source. The provision states, 'The accuracy of the content and source of any programme to be transmitted shall be ascertained.' Even if the duty of disclosing the source is not explicitly

44. More on the necessity of protecting journalistic sources, *see* UNESCO (2017), *Protecting Journalistic Sources in the Digital Age, UNESCO Series on Internet Freedom*, http://unesdoc.unesco.org/images/0024/002480/248054E.pdf (accessed 21 Feb. 2018).

demanded, the fact that the journalist is duty bound to ascertain the source and its accuracy entails disclosure of the original source. In light of such a stringent condition, the Ethiopian approach deviates from the internationally accentuated standard not only on its failure to legally protect the confidentiality of journalistic sources but also on its deteriorated stand of shifting the burden on the journalist to ascertain the accuracy of the information, and by compelling to disclose its source.

164. Likewise, Article 2047 of the general Civil Code – one of the provisions that regulate cases of defamation charges which may result in tort (extra-contractual) liability – also resembles to condone the significance of protecting a journalistic source. If the defendant, i.e., in this case, the journalist is to escape a civil liability on charges of defamation, he/she would have to adduce proof of the accuracy of the alleged facts and that he/she had not acted solely to injure the plaintiff. This condition inevitably requires disclosure of the original source, and hence, the fundamental value of protecting journalistic source cannot be invoked as a justification to refute the charge with no need to verify the truthfulness of the allegations by revealing the source.

165. Somehow, the Criminal Code – a law conventionally known for its prohibitive and punitive character – appears, at least in principle, to sensitise the value of protecting a journalistic source. Article 45 of the Code, titled 'secrecy of the identity of a source' initially sets the principle under paragraph 1 stating that 'the editor or publisher of any publication, which is not periodical, may not be compelled to disclose the name or pen-name of the author'. Scope wise, the protection remains incomplete as it does not include periodicals in which case the right to keep confidential of the contributor or the author cannot be asserted by the editor or the publisher. Additionally, it prevents only the compulsory disclosure of the name or pen name of the author, and hence, not other aspects of the publication. In light of this, paragraph 1 of Article 45 needs to be recited jointly with paragraph 2 which is more ubiquitously articulated with a straightforward aim of protecting a journalistic source. Accordingly, as per paragraph 2, 'the publisher or editor of any publication [in this case, including periodicals alike] may not be compelled to disclose the source of any matter printed in publication'.

166. Reading the more inclusive protective aspect of paragraph 2, from the outset, it might seem tempting to argue that Article 45 of the Criminal Code has guaranteed the required level of legal protection against disclosure of journalistic sources. Revisiting this notion in the context of the exceptions as provided under paragraph 3 of the same Article 45 of the Code, however, would reveal the inescapable vulnerability of the protection. This is mainly because, the protection to a journalistic source may not preclude the court from compelling the publisher or the editor to disclose the information if a crime is adjudged to have been committed either against the constitutional order, the national defence force or against the security of the State constituting a clear and imminent danger. Furthermore, the status and decisiveness of the information in the case of proceedings of a serious crime to such an extent that the source does not have other alternatives to prove the case would also justify its mandatory disclosure notwithstanding its character as a journalistic source.

167. Indeed, given that the legal protection of journalistic source cannot be absolute, imposing some legitimate exceptions against such a privilege may not be problematic in and of itself. The scenarios and the circumstances under which Article 45(3) of the Code justified compulsory disclosure of journalistic source, however, undermines the entire notion that necessitated to vindicate the protection paradigm. For one thing, it is not clearly stated whether the scope and purpose of the obligatory disclosure of the information relate only for alleged media-related crimes or in connection to every crime that a journalistic work might have relevancy in dealing with the case. Additionally, the political nature of the crimes invoked as circumstances justifying the forceful disclosure of journalistic source would unavoidably expose the very subjectivity-prone depiction of Article 45(3) in its practical application. There lacks precision in regards to the nature and elements of a crime to constitute as an offence against the constitutional order; as a crime against the National Defence Force; or as an offence against the Security of the State.

168. Similar ambiguities as to the meaning of a 'serious crime' as postulated under Article 45(3(b)) are also likely to invite arbitrariness in legitimising unnecessary disclosure of journalistic sources. For that matter, even if Article 45(3(b)) requires to establish the impossibility of substantiating the case through any other alternative source before compelling the publisher or the editor demanding for disclosure, there is no lucidity as the procedural or technical requisites in establishing whether there exists a genuine claim of such an instance. The question of who owes the onus to prove the absence of any other alternative source in corroborating the case remains unsettled.

169. Generally, notwithstanding the value of Article 45(1 & 2) in setting the normative basis in all arguments substantiating the positive stand of the law towards ensuring confidentiality of journalistic sources, in light of these obscurities, however, it would be naïve to not remain sceptical of such an enigmatically formulated standard falling short of upholding the essence of the protection.

170. Tellingly, such a loosely construed normative approach in protecting journalistic sources, and rather the directive duty imposed on journalists to disclose their sources, appears to have exposed the quality of journalistic works in the country. As documented in the study conducted by Human Rights Watch, journalists contend that 'it has become increasingly difficult to find witnesses to events and experts who are willing to be interviewed from inside Ethiopia'.[45] Such reluctance to cooperate with the media mainly stems from the fear of speaking out on sensitive issues which might result in multifaceted threats, harassments, and detentions.[46] Accordingly, if

45. Human Rights Watch, *Journalism is Not a Crime: Violations of Media Freedom in Ethiopia*, https://www.hrw.org/sites/default/files/reports/ethiopia0115_ForUploadR.pdf (accessed 22 Feb. 2018).
46. *Ibid.*

the print media in general and journalists, in particular, are to have any prospect in serving the public as a vibrant and genuine custodian of public matters through their capacity as watchdogs of daily state-society interactions, the country needs more pragmatically formulated legislative safeguards to journalistic sources.

Chapter 3. Journalists' Liability

§1. General Information on the Liability System

171. Involvement in a journalistic work ensues not only rights and privileges as defining elements of the profession, it also supervenes accountability if it contravenes the legally prescribed limitations justified on legitimate grounds. The liability springs from the generally vindicated restrictions applicable in the broader context of the right to freedom of speech, and the unique position and function of a journalist as the heartbeat for the smooth flow of ideas – the seeking, receiving, and imparting – in the market. In other words, as freedom of expression is not an absolute right which may be subjected to legitimate restraints, so is a journalist work which is highly reliant on the margin of the legal protection accorded to the freedom of speech. Accordingly, once a journalist is adjudged to have crossed the permissible professional margin protected by the law, then follows a liability for his/her action or inaction depending on the circumstances of the case.

172. As briefly noted in the first part of the monograph, a range of proclamations that regulate the Ethiopian media landscape enclose provisions of a punitive character. The measures to be taken in pursuance to these provisions could be characterised as administrative, civil or criminal culpabilities. While the majority of the measures articulated target the journalist as an individual duty bearer depending on his/her specific role, there are also actions directed at entities, such as publishers or distributors. Regarding the nature of liability, while some measures such as the imposition of fines, revocation or suspension of license, or confiscation of journalistic materials are less intrusive, a journalist may also face either simple or rigorous imprisonments upon conviction on criminal charges related to his/her journalistic work. Having these general backdrops as a point of departure, an in-depth analysis of the specific aspects of liabilities is discussed in the sections that follow focussing on the pertinent provisions of the Press Proclamation No. 590/2008.

§2. The Principles of Liabilities

173. Before delving into the specific actions stipulated in the Proclamation, the guiding principles that dictate the application of these penalties are worth of a particular comment. Albeit not unequivocally titled as principles, and not even specifically mentioning 'journalists' as holders of such a protection, Article 39 of the Press Proclamation embodies what may be called as 'the principle of supremacy of public interest' as a defence against any liability for disclosing a certain information. Paragraph 2 of the provision states:

> No one may be subject to any legal, administrative or employment-related sanction, regardless of any breach of a legal or employment obligation, for releasing information on wrongdoing, or which would disclose a serious threat to health, safety or the environment, as long as he acted in good faith and in

the reasonable belief that the information was substantially true and disclosed evidence of wrongdoing or a serious threat to health, safety or the environment.

Before analysing the content of the text, it needs to be noted from the outset that Article 39 is placed under part three of the Proclamation which regulates the substantial and procedural notions administering the right of access to information. Reading the provision standing from the section where it is cemented might lead to contemplate the narrow-in-scope application of the provision only in the context of the public relation officer's conduct, and as a safeguard against the consequences of his/her decisions either in sanctioning or rejecting the release of a certain information that belongs to a public body as defined in the Proclamation.[47] This said, looking at the substantial essence of the text, there can be no logical narration that precludes its application as a normative base in protecting journalists from unwarranted administrative, civil or criminal liabilities as consequences of their works that disclose certain information in the course of performing their watchdogging role to the best interest of the public.

174. Reading Article 39(2) in light of this broader submission, no journalist shall be subjected to administrative, civil or criminal sanction for disclosing a certain information when the release of such information serves to one of the purposes specified therein. Most importantly, this protection cannot be justified on grounds his/her decision of disclosing the information is a breach of a legal or employment obligation given that public interest should override in all the circumstances the case. Accordingly, as long as the journalist acted in good faith and in reasonable belief as to the truthfulness of the information, disclosing it to the public in order to expose wrongdoing, a serious threat to societal health, safety and the environment shall not result in any liability no matter whether exists a prior legal or contractual obligation to keep the confidentiality of the information. Indeed, that is what a more commendable job of a journalist desperately required be; a task which should not be compromised in so far as public interest is involved in it.

175. Paragraph 3 of Article 39 further supplements the notion by providing definitional precision, of what constitutes a 'wrongdoing'. The term is intended to refer to the disclosure of acts of criminal offences, failures to comply with legal obligations, exposing a miscarriage of justice, corruption, dishonesty, abuse of power or serious misconduct. These are sensitive matters of public interest whereby investigative journalists, in particular, are ought to dedicate their time, skill and resources if the ever-demanding values of justice, rule of law, accountability, transparency, and good governance are to be instilled in all aspects of democratic societal change that the country is craving for.

---

47. Article 2(5) of the Press Proclamation defines 'public body' as 'anybody established under the Federal Constitution or state constitution or any other law which forms part of any level or branch of the federal or regional state or owned, controlled or directly or indirectly substantially financed by funds provided by the federal or regional governments or accountable to the federal or regional states'.

176. Nonetheless, such a prospect may hold true, only if provisions such as Article 39 are implemented in the manner that provides the utmost legal protection to journalists' professional commitment instead of subjecting them to sanctions of various types. In light of this demand, the interpretation and practical application of the provisions that impose the various sanctions as punitive measures against journalists should, therefore, be guided by this general protection and to the narrowest possible extent the aim of which should only be to prevent some aggravated abuses of the profession. Having such a general backdrop in mind, the different forms of liabilities stipulated under the Ethiopian Press Proclamation are briefly highlighted hereunder.

I. Administrative Measures

177. In this section, an administrative measure is portrayed as a measure taken by a body other than the court. These are actions mostly executed by the EBA on its mandate as a monitoring or supervisory body of the country's media outlets. As previously outlined, the Authority is mandated to issue a license and supervise not only of the broadcast media but also the print media.[48]

178. Accordingly, suspending or cancelling a certificate of registration or license could be cited as the most prominent administrative measure. As clearly provided under Article 7(2) of the Broadcast Proclamation, the Authority is entitled to suspend or cancel the license of a periodical. Moreover, aside from the practical challenges in controlling abuses in the exercise of such a power, pursuant to Article 7(5) of the Proclamation, the Authority is entrusted to control illegal transmissions in the broadcast media, and hence illegal publication and distribution of periodicals in the print media.

179. More specific to suspending the distribution of print media outlets is the public prosecutor's power of impounding periodicals and books as provided for in Article 42 of the Press Proclamation. As per paragraph 2 of this Article, a public prosecutor – the federal or regional prosecutor depending on the case – may issue an order of impounding a periodical or a book which is about to be disseminated if he/she has sufficient reason to believe that it contains illegal matter, which would if disseminated, lead to a clear and present grave danger to national security which could not otherwise be averted through a subsequent imposition of sanctions. Such a measure remains as an administrative action so long as it was made without a prior court order, or at least until the time that such a measure is retrospectively endorsed by the court or until a criminal proceeding is instituted. In this aspect, non-judicial impoundment of a periodical or a book can be considered as one of the typical administrative measures that a journalist may have to encounter as a punitive action against his/her journalist work.

48. *See supra* the section on Registration of the print media.

180. The other liability that may fall into the category of administrative measure is the duty to correct and publish free of charge, any reply to any factual information or matter which is claimed to be injurious to the honour and reputation of another person. Here again, Article 40 of the Press Proclamation ensures the right to reply, of any person who asserts his honour and reputation being affected by the publication. As clearly dictated in the subsequent sub-paragraphs of Article 40(1), in so far as the complainant and the mass media have reached into a consensus for the publication of a reply, there is no need for a court order to that effect. Article 40(2–7) invites judicial intervention on the matter only after the refusal by the mass media to entertain the demand of the complainant for the insertion and publication of the reply. Hence, until the case reaches that stage, it remains a liability of an administrative nature.

II. Criminal Liabilities

181. Of the most serious action a journalist may encounter on the ground of his/her journalistic work is a criminal culpability, the consequence upon conviction of which may be either/both imprisonment or/and the payment of fines. As meticulously addressed somewhere in Part II of the monograph, a range of legislation – chiefly that of the general Criminal Code and the Anti-Terrorism Proclamation – have prescribed variety of media and speech-related offences, in pursuance of which several journalists have been targeted and imprisoned. This section, however, focuses only on the relevant provisions of the Press Proclamation and attempts to summarise the grounds for, the nature and the degree of penalties upon conviction on the crimes proscribed therein.

182. To begin, Article 41 of the Press Proclamation establishes the rule in regards to the identity the person responsible for the crimes. Accordingly, for a criminal offence committed through the media, both the media establishment and the individual person (the journalist) may jointly be held accountable. This joinder of criminal liability is further tightened under Article 46 of the Code which commands that no juridical person shall escape criminal liability either alone or jointly with any individual criminals listed under Articles 43–45 of the Code.

183. Coming to the liability of individual persons depending on their specific role, Article 43(1) of the general Criminal Code stipulates the circumstances under which the editor-in-chief, the publisher, the printer, the disseminator, or the importer held criminally liable for offences committed through the publication of periodicals. First of all, the editor-in-chief assumes the principal criminal responsibility if the periodical was registered. But if the periodical was not licensed by the time of its publication; or if the editor-in-chief no longer qualifies or has ceased to function in his/her role; or if the editor-in-chief was appointed merely for the sake of appearance or was otherwise manifestly not in a position of exercising his/her powers by the time of the publication of the periodical, then the publisher becomes criminally accountable in pursuance to Article 43(1(b & c)) of the Criminal Code. Then comes the liability of the printer, in which case it has to be adduced that establishing the identity of the publisher by the time of publication of the periodical was impossible. Still, if it becomes unmanageable to ascertain the identity of the printer, or if it was found to be incorrect, then the disseminator becomes liable in lieu of the printer. Finally, there comes liability in relation to periodicals imported from abroad. In this case, either the importer – but not the person who imported the periodical for his/her own personal use – or the disseminator are held liable.

184. On the other hand, the Code under Article 43(2) provides a separate list of accountable persons for crimes committed on printed materials other than a periodical. At this point the author becomes liable, but only if: (i) he/she has been named as an author of the printed matter; (ii) his/her name, pen name or pseudonym appeared in the publication securing his/her wish; and (iii) the material was published with his/her consent. Then if it was not possible to establish the liability of an individual author for a printed matter which includes contributions by several authors, then the responsible editor nominated in a manner prescribed by law (if any) undertakes the liability. If, however, neither the author nor the editor could be held liable for all the possible reasons as for provided under Article 43(2(e)), the publisher shall assume the responsibility. The same order of liability follows the printer and finally the distributor according to the circumstances of the case.

185. Last but not the least to be noted in regard to the identity of persons and the order of their criminal liability is the prohibition of double liability as provided for under Article 46 of the Criminal Code. That is, no criminal liability can be imposed on different persons for the same crime so that the punishment of one of the parties in the order of their accountability automatically excludes the punishment of the other parties for the same conduct. This said, as for provided under Article 41(1) of the Press Proclamation, the prohibition of double liability does not, however, exempt the media establishment from incurring a joint criminal liability alongside the responsible person.

186. For heuristic purposes, depending on the actual nature of the conduct, the (print) media-related offences may be categorised into two. The relatively less contestable category are offences committed in breach of the legally imposed conditions for the lawful ownership and operation of the print media. These are mainly contraventions to the formality and administrative requisites as prescribed under Article 45 of the Press Proclamation that result penalties in the form of a fine. A breach, for example, of the media ownership related restrictions as set forth under Article 7 of the Press Proclamation would amount as a violation of the law with a corresponding penalty of up to 200,000 Ethiopian Birr as a fine. In the same vein, failure to appoint the responsible editor for a periodical as per Article 6(1 & 2); non-compliance with the obligations stipulated under Article 9(6); or violating the obligations as provided under Article 10 of the Press Proclamation also amount to infringement of the law and is punishable with fine up to 15,000 Ethiopian Birr.

187. The other category of media-related offences are the more egregious ordinary crimes allegedly committed using the mass media as a communicative landscape for the materialisation of the crime. Article 42 of the Criminal Code defines these offences echoing:

> crimes relating to the mass media are those which are committed by means of *newspapers, books, leaflets, journals, posters, pictures*, cinemas, radio or television broadcasting or any other means of the mass media. [emphasis added].

Further elaborating the moment at which the commission of these crimes is deemed to have been actually materialised, Article 42(3) demands the requirement of establishing the fact that the matter has been essentially communicated to the public. Accordingly, no media-related crime is reckoned to have been committed at an earlier stage before the message reaches to the public. While determining this fact which triggers the criminal liability of the person, Article 43(5) of the Code cements an irrevocable presumption to the effect that the content of the matter communicated to the public through the mass media is deemed to have been inserted, published or disseminated with the knowledge and consent of the person in charge of such a task.

188. Apart from that, Article 42 also identifies the potential victims of media-related crimes which could be either against persons and their honour; against the public or private safety; or against any other legal right protected by criminal law.

189. Minding these general principles in the course of establishing elements of any crime committed through the print media, both the Criminal Code under Article 44, and Articles 41 and 43 of the Press Proclamation have made inventories of the potential specific crimes the person – the journalist for this particular section – would likely be accountable for either as principal, as instigator or as an accomplice depending on the weight given to his/her participation in the commission of the alleged crime. Accordingly, a person who contributed either as an author, originator or publisher of the diffused or published matter is deemed to have taken part in the commission of crimes namely: armed rising or civil war (Article 240); treason (Articles 248–250); espionage (Article 252); attempted incitement and assistance (Article 255); provocation and preparation (Article 257); crimes against humanity (Articles 269–274); incitement to disregard military order (Article 332); disclosure of military secrets (Article 336); breaches of military and official secrecy (Articles 396 & 397); inciting the public through false rumours (Article 486(b)) of the Criminal Code; or any deliberate disregard of an obligation to maintain secrecy specified by any other law. Noting the nature of these crimes – which are not only serious as crimes deemed committed against the public and the state but also in light of the rigorous character of the punishments attached to the offences that include death penalty or life imprisonment – the criminal liability of a journalist could perhaps be one of the most egregious criminal law response to offences allegedly committed in the mass media.

190. Moreover, as briefly abridged in Part II of the monograph, the Criminal Code also prescribes other media-related petty offences, or crimes committed against private individuals or organisations, the prosecution of which will necessitate a personal complaint to be lodged by the alleged victim.

191. In a similar vein, the Press Proclamation also appears to extend journalists' criminal liability mainly from two interrelated aspects. On the one hand, Article 43(7) of the Proclamation introduces the thickest essence of criminal defamation by adducing rather absurd offences of false accusations and defamation against the so-called constitutionally established legislative, executive and judicial authorities. On the other, even if one may argue invoking the need to protect the names or honour of officials from defamatory or false accusations, no specific threshold is explicitly provided by the Proclamation in order to differentiate false accusations and defamations that are directed against the official as an individual and those directed at the office run by the individual authority. The law is not even clear whether the false accusation or the defamatory statement against the official disseminated through the media should cover matters related only to his/her official duties and responsibilities, or it also includes issues pertaining to his/her private or personal matter. Generally, noting that state officials and public offices should be the ones that a journalistic work must supposedly prioritise in scrutinising their (dis-)functions and (in)actions – which, in essence define the fate of issues of public interest in a democratic society – empowering the public prosecutor to file criminal charges of false accusation or defamation on behalf of an official, even with no need for the latter's prior compliant, would amount nothing but altering the natural public duty of the prosecutor in the criminal litigation into that of a private legal counsel representing the individual interest of an individual official. Such an approach may not enhance the watchdogging role of journalistic work, and at worst it would pose a serious threat against the proper exercising of the role.

192. The Press Proclamation has reformed not only some substantial aspects of crimes related to the mass media but also other procedural matters relevant in the course of administrating the litigation. At least in principle, the Proclamation appears to address some of the procedural standards that the general Criminal Procedure Code has overlooked to deal with. Chief among these changes is the manner in which a criminal charge is supposed to be initiated and the reasonable time within which the case has to be adjudicated by the court. To begin with, at the outset the proclamation resembles to demand that no action of remanding the person suspected of committing an offence through the mass media for further investigation is required to bring him/her to the court. Article 43(1) of the Proclamation, however, falls short of absolutely prohibiting pre-charge or investigative detention of the suspect as the discretion towards this effect is fully vested to the attorney general. Neither the circumstances that may justify the general attorney's decision for remand are enumerated nor is there an explicitly stated right to challenge the remand.

193. The other time-based procedural advancement relates to the period within which the court shall commence the hearing and pronounce its judgment on the case. Accordingly, Article 43(2) demands the court to commence the hearing within fifteen days as of the date of filing the criminal charge. Such a compulsory period of a specified number of days for the hearing of the case will minimise unnecessary pretrial delays and irregularities, which augments the suspect's right to prompt judicial review of his/her case. Furthermore, as an essential component of the suspect's right to be promptly informed of the charge and the evidence brought in substantiating the charge, which is irreplaceably vital in defending his/her case, Article 43(3) entails the court to ensure that the suspect obtains the copy of the charge and other evidence (if any), at least five days before the commencement of the hearing. Then comes the procedural right to speedy trial. Hence, as for provided under Article 43(4), once the hearing commences, the court shall render judgment within one month on the merit of the case.

194. The parties' right to appeal is also strictly regulated under Article 44 of the Proclamation, and all the necessary measures to be taken at the appellate court are time-bounded. As a point of departure, the aggrieved party may lodge a memorandum of appeal to the appellate court within thirty days after the judgment by the trial court is rendered. Aiming to avoid further delays at this stage, the appellate court is then expected to give the copies of the appeal to the other party within twenty-four hours of receiving such a notice for appeal. On its part, the appellate court shall give its decision on the matter within ten days of receiving the appeal.

195. Generally, noting all the afore-highlighted specific-time-bounded durations that the concerned party is required to comply with both at the trial and appellate court litigations, it can be submitted that the Ethiopian Press Proclamation has put an unprecedented and exemplary setup for the better enforcement of prompt and speedy trial administration. Alas, these and related normative advancements do not seem to have brought to an end, of the long-standing deficiencies of the criminal justice system which is predominantly characterised by unwarranted investigative detentions, unduly prolonged criminal litigations, and adjournments. Perhaps as one notable ground, the more draconically crafted rules of the anti-terrorism proclamation have been predominantly invoked as proffered regulatory frameworks on similar procedural matters so that these innovative aspects of the Press Proclamation are being practically overshadowed or effectually muted in their application.

196. The final point when it comes to the procedure is the rule on the period of limitation. Here again, deviating from the general statute of limitations provided under Articles 215–222 of the Criminal Code, Article 46 of the Press Proclamation has restricted the time. Thus, no criminal proceeding for an offence committed through a periodical may be initiated one year after the publication of the offending matter. The exception to this limitation is only if the person is suspected of committing crimes against humanity the prosecution of which shall not be barred by any statute of limitation as for provided under Article 28(1) of the Constitution.

III. Civil Liabilities for Defamation

197. Apart from the criminal liability one may have to encounter upon conviction for defamation, both the general Civil Code and the Press Proclamation have also imposed a civil, i.e., extra-contractual liability against the defendant, which is normally due in the form of compensation. A civil action against the defendant on the ground a defamatory statement in any form – be it libel which is made in writing, or slander which is committed through oral speech – may be instituted regardless of his/her conviction or otherwise acquittal on the criminal charge brought against the same conduct. Hence, as set forth both under Article 2149 of the Civil Code and Article 41(4) of the Press Proclamation, the right to claim damages for a mass media offence of defamation may not be scrapped on the ground of the criminal court's decision of acquitting or discharging the suspect.

198. The Press Proclamation has also set a separate period of limitation when it comes to a claim for damage caused by the mass media which is to be brought in a civil court. Accordingly, even if the possibility to file a criminal prosecution of defamation is barred by a statute of limitation, this same fact may not preclude the plaintiff's right to claim the damage to be made good through compensation. What is not addressed in the Proclamation is, however, the question of which law would govern the applicable statute of limitation on civil matters pertaining to claims for damage caused by the print mass media which are brought to a civil court after the lapse of the period to institute a criminal prosecution against the same conduct in a criminal court? That is the one-year period of limitation in relation to offences committed through a periodical as provided under Article 46(1) of the Press Proclamation. Certainly, by the mere fact that the Proclamation allows the right to claim compensation for a damage caused by a defamatory statement even after the lapse of the period for a criminal prosecution would not imply as if it grants a timeless privilege to initiate such a civil action as every right is deemed to have been renounced if it is not exercised within a certain period of time. Given that the claim is to rely on the relevant section of the Civil Code that governs tort-based liabilities, one alternative to fill such a gap would be referring the statute of limitation as for provided under Article 2143(1) of the Code, which requires the victim to bring an action for compensation within two years from the time at which he/she suffered the damage.

199. Coming to the substantial elements that need to be ascertained in order for a certain statement to constitute as an act of defamation, the relevant provisions of the Civil Code (Articles 2044–2049) may have to be methodically consulted. Accordingly, as a point of departure, Article 2044 cements the definitional principle stating:

> a person commits an offence where by his words, his writings, or by any other means he acts in such a way as to make another living person detestable, contemptible, or ridiculous and to jeopardise his credit, his reputation, or his future.

From the definition, three basic elements must be exhaustively established: a conduct of the person reflected in his statement through words (slander) or writings (libel) or any other medium; the effect of such a conduct in making another living person (victim) despicable, disgraceful, and ludicrous; as a result of which his/her credit, reputation and future becomes jeopardised. Having such a definitional threshold in principle, the provisions that follow have stipulated the possible exceptions and the extent to which these exemptions may justify the defendant's conduct. Most notably, matters of public interest, proving the truth of the alleged fact, the need to ensure unrestrained parliamentary debates and judicial proceedings are generally discounted from the definitional domain so that no civil liability is ought to be incurred.

200. Once an act of defamation is established in a civil proceeding for the purpose of making the moral damage good through compensation, the circumstances which may justify compensation for moral damage, and the maximum amount the court may order the defendant to pay, are respectively stipulated under Articles 2109 of the Civil Code and Article 41(2) of the Press Proclamation. In principle, therefore, either the plaintiff may be awarded a fair compensation by way of redress or the defendant may be ordered to pay the amount to a charity organisation designated by the plaintiff. In regards to the possible amount of compensation to be claimed, Article 41(2) of the Press Proclamation affixes a maximum of 100,000 Ethiopian Birr as the highest margin of payment the court may award depending on the seriousness of the moral damage caused to the plaintiff. At this point, the hardest task of the court would be to define what constitutes a serious moral damage, and which types of defamatory statements are likely to trigger such a damage, in order for the court to objectively assess the defendant's particular conduct. Arguably, the circumstances listed under Article 2109 are of directly important in assisting the court's task of ascertaining the degree of the damage and the corresponding judgement on the amount of compensation. In light of this, if the injurious or defamatory statement are of allegations: that the plaintiff has committed a crime punishable under the criminal law; that the plaintiff is incompetent or dishonest in the exercise of his/her profession; that the plaintiff – if a businessman – is insolvent; that the plaintiff is suffering from a contagious disease; or that the plaintiff is of low morals, then the court may have to award a fair compensation in due consideration of the impact of these statements in tarnishing the credit, honour and future of the plaintiff.

Chapter 4. Right to Reply

201. Basically aimed at rectifying false information disseminated through mass media, or at times, as a duty of the mass media to create an accessible platform for the alleged victim to present his/her version of the story concerning the disputed information, the right to reply is regarded as one of the common means of remedying some deliberate or unintended mistakes made in a journalistic work. Accordingly, the right to reply is an entitlement to refute by a person whose honour or reputation is deemed to have been damaged because of certain factual information or a matter disseminated through the mass media.

202. The recognition of the right to reply and the purpose it protects have been regulated in different legal systems[49] and the Ethiopian media legislation does not seem an exception to such a trend. To that end, Articles 40 and 45(4) of the Press Proclamation, Article 42 of the Broadcasting Proclamation, and Article 2049 of the general Civil Code are of the most pertinent provisions that regulate the essence of the right and its enforcement in the Ethiopian mass media. As a normative backup to the right, Article 40(1) of the Press Proclamation states:

> where any factual information or matter injurious to the honour or reputation of any person is reported in a mass media, such a person shall have the right to have his reply inserted, free of charge in the publication in which the report appeared.

Besides its value in the course of addressing the issue of who holds the right – i.e., the person whose reputation or honour is claimed to have been affected by the information reported in the mass media – the provision also dictates the manner in which the concerned duty bearer has to act upon the request. To begin with, the reply has to be accepted free of charge. Second, it must be inserted and published in a publication through which the disputed information initially appeared or disseminated.

203. The subsequent paragraphs of Article 40 further regulate the required standards, the procedure, and the duration within which the requested reply has to be administered. As the principal duty bearer, the editor or his/her deputy assumes the responsibility to publish any reply addressed to him/her. In so doing, neither a publication charge shall be requested nor should the content of the reply be subject to correction.

204. Timewise, the reply must be published as expeditiously as possible depending on the type of the publication. In this regard, whereas the reply has to be published within three days after the reception of the request if the publication is a daily newspaper, the same request should be issued within nine days of receipt when the publication is a weekly newspaper. The three-day period to entertain the person's

49. *See also* Youm Kyu Ho, *The Right of Reply and Freedom of the Press: An International and Comparative Perspective*, 76 *George Washington Law Rev.* 1017–1064 (2008).

right to reply in a daily newspaper is further reduced only to twenty-four hours if the disputed information was disseminated during the election process. In any other publications, publishing the reply in the upcoming issue that appears after receiving the request is deemed to fulfil the requirement of promptness in enforcing the person's right to reply. On the other hand, a slightly extended time-span is provided when the information that triggered a reply is disseminated through a broadcast media, which could be either radio or television. In such a case, Article 40(1(b)) requires the responsible programme editor to insert the reply in the next part of the programme or in other similar programmes within fourteen days of the receipt. In a similar fashion, while the fourteen-day period is reduced in to forty-eight hours if the information that has given rise to the reply was disseminated during election period, the prohibition of correcting the content of the reply and charging a fee for the publication are equally applicable for replies made in the broadcast media.

205. The other aspect relates to the standardised content of the reply. As clearly narrated under Article 40(1(c)) of the Press Proclamation, any reply should fulfil the requirements of proportionality with, and relevant in refuting the disputed information, and has to be lawful in its content. Accordingly, the right to reply does not guarantee unrestricted and limitless right of response from the aggrieved person. The other restriction on the right to reply would be the statute of limitation as for provided under Article 40(5) of the Press Proclamation. Hence, any request for an insertion of a reply has to be made within three months from the day on which the disputed information was reported or disseminated. Accordingly, any demand for a reply after the three-month period would be barred by a period of limitation.

206. In terms of procedure, at a first glance, implementing the right to reply may be characterised as an administrative setup which is resumes through a direct dialogue between the person and the responsible editor or the deputy. Only when such a direct administrative request is proved fruitless upon refusal to comply by the chief editor, the person may bring the matter to the court seeking for compulsory insertion of the reply in the periodical or in the broadcast programme as a remedy to be sought. Once a petition to this effect is submitted, the court has to render judgment within the following ten days in the normal circumstances, and within twenty-four hours during the election process. The consequence depends on the outcome of the court's judgment on the case. If the court finds the refusal inappropriate, the chief editor or the other responsible person in the order as for provided under Article 43 of the Criminal Code shall be held liable for penalties. The maximum amount of the penalty is precisely cemented under Article 45(3) of the Press Proclamation, which may extend up to 15,000 Ethiopian Birr. While assessing the liability, however, the court shall give due regard to the justifications stipulated under Article 2049 of the general Civil Code.

207. The Press Proclamation recognises not only the right to reply but also the person's right to correct any mistakenly reported factual information regarding him/her. As to the standards, the procedure, and statute of limitation, the same provisions discussed hitherto are deemed mutatis mutandis applicable to enforce the right to correct erroneous information.

208. Somehow intersected concepts are actions withdrawal and publication of apology by the defendant who committed defamation by way of publication but without any intention to injure the plaintiff or with no gross negligence. As submitted under Article 2049 of the Civil Code, such a formal action of withdrawal and publication of apology accepting the mistakes made in the publication would exempt the defendant's liability for compensation. The withdrawal and the apology may be published in a periodical of his choice if the defamation was committed by way of a periodical which appears at intervals of more than once in a week. In other cases, the withdrawal or apology can be published in the periodical in which the defamatory statement was initially disseminated.

209. Generally, the right to reply on a disputed information and the right to correct erroneous information about the person on the one hand as actions to be taken by the plaintiff and actions of withdrawal and formal apologies as rectifying measures by the defendant on the other are all given legal recognition under the afore-highlighted relevant provisions of the laws of the country.

Chapter 5. Access to Public Information

210. As discussed in Part I, the freedom to seek and access public information is an important element in the practical enjoyment of freedom of expression and opinion. It is almost a truism that access to public information is helpful to formulate an opinion and to reflect upon matters of public interest. From the journalistic professional point of view, in a system whereby access to public information is perceived as merely a luxurious dispensation to which only a few elites hold the key to access it and make it accessible upon their discretion, the watchdog role of journalism, investigative journalism, and the inherent function of the mass media as architects of public dialogue would languish simply as theoretical yearnings. Accordingly, its significance in promoting democracy, in enhancing good governance, and in maintaining transparent and accountable leadership highly relies on the normative and institutional guarantees that the right is accorded in a given legal system.

211. Leaving aside pro tem the normative details that are likely to threaten the proper implementation of the right – a subject to be addressed later in this chapter –, the Ethiopian Freedom of the Mass Media and Access to Information Proclamation [the Press Proclamation] appears to restate the aforesaid values of ensuring the right to access to public information. Indeed, more than two-thirds of the provisions of the Proclamation are devoted to cement the rules governing the enforcement of the right. Intriguingly, much of the preambular paragraphs are also strongly articulated with particular emphasis to the rationales that necessitate apposite legislative guarantees enhancing the exercise of the right. Paragraph 7 of the preamble, for example, reiterates the need to recognise:

> the right of the media to collect and disseminate information, including of a critical nature; realizing that an independent mass media that serves as a public forum for uninhibited democratic dialogue thrives on a viable freedom of information system that facilitates the free flow of information and ideas among citizens by enabling them to exercise their right to seek, receive and impart information and opinions freely.

212. The Proclamation also vows to reaffirm the fundamental importance of the right of individuals to access information held by public bodies for the betterment of democratic and transparent conduct of governmental affairs. Reaffirming its determination to promote the values of accountability and transparency in the conduct of public affairs, the Proclamation further accentuates the need to impose a legal obligation on public officials to facilitate access to individuals and the mass media to information so that matters of public interest may be disclosed and discussed publicly. With this general introductory remark in mind, the broader question of whether the pertinent provisions of the Proclamation genuinely reflect these vehemently asserted aspirations of the law is reviewed in different sections presented as follows.

§1. Public Documents and Meetings

213. Before delving into the procedural and circumstantial aspects in the enforcement of the right, the substantial-content-focused issue of what is to be accessed may necessitate the task of determining the scope of the right. It is indisputable that the object of the right is information, but not every information is subject to the rules that demand its accessibility. In its normative sense, Article 2(6) of the Press Proclamation defines information as 'any material recorded in any form'. That said, the type of information which becomes the undisputable object of the individual's right to access is the one that is typified as a public information. The other segment, i.e., personal information, on the other hand, is mainly protected by the laws dealing with the right to privacy, and hence its reachability is beyond the scope of the right to access to information. Plainly speaking, therefore, it is only public information that falls within the scope and subject matter of the right.

214. As to the notion of what constitutes public information, Article 2(7) of the Proclamation appears to define the concept stating 'as any recorded information in a possession and under the control of a public body' – a body as described under Article 2(5) of the Proclamation – but no matter by whom and when it was actually created. Apart from that, the information may be in any format or medium such as a document, file, manuscript, microfilm, microfiche, facsimile, or reproduced images. Note has to be taken, however, that information in the hands of a public body may not always be portrayed as public information as there remains a possibility that the concerned public body may – in pursuance to its functions, duties and responsibilities conferred to it by law – still be in custody of private information.

215. Seemingly with an intent to provide further precision to the content of the right, Article 2(8) opts to narrate illustrative lists of records to be characterised as personal information about an identifiable individual. In this regard, records relating to the medical, educational, professional, employment, criminal, or financial transactions made by the individual are typified as personal information. Furthermore, the ethnic, national or social origin of the person, his/her marital status, sexual orientation, colour, age, pregnancy, physical or mental health condition, well-being, disability, religion, culture, language, belief, conciseness, or birth of the individual are also placed under the same category of personal information. In addition, any information regarding any identifying number, symbol, address, blood type, fingerprint, or other particulars assigned to the individual also belongs to this category. Likewise, the personal views, opinions, and preferences of the individual that has nothing to do with the interest of another person, as well as the views or opinions of an unidentified person about the individual are also considered as personal information.

216. To sum up, public information, as it stands in the Ethiopian Press Proclamation, can be defined as information other than personal information about an identifiable individual, and which is possessed and controlled by a public body. With this understanding in regards to the subject matter of the right, the relevant section of the Proclamation which sets the principle as to the normative protection of the right and the exceptions, as well as the main objectives intended to be achieved through the rules governing its implementation are briefly assessed hereunder.

217. Part Three of the Press Proclamation, which covers the main body of the instrument, contains about thirty provisions aimed at governing the various issues that may arise in the course of implementing the right.

218. In so doing, it starts under Article 11 by cementing the main objectives of the rules stipulated thereunder. Actually, a careful reading of the content of Article 11 would reveal not only its value as an objective statement but also as an interpretational parameter and as a lensing tool based on which the rest of the provisions has to be construed and implemented accordingly. Hence, even if the non-absolute character of the right is undisputed, the ultimate target of the rules should only be ensuring the right of citizens to access, receive, and impart information held by public bodies. To that end, the vitality of establishing proper mechanisms and procedures that could best give effect to the right in a manner which enables persons to obtain information as quickly, inexpensively, and effortlessly as is reasonably possible, is unequivocally surfaced. Besides, the interpretation of the provisions and the extent of their practical application should always be guided by the ultimate gauges of their assenting influence in promoting public participation and empowerment, in promoting good governance, in nurturing the culture of transparency, accountability, and efficiency in the functions of public bodies.

219. Article 11 also pinpoints the overriding public and private interests, according to the circumstances of each case, as the only legitimate grounds that may justify limitations in the exercising of the right. The Proclamation further extends the necessity of prioritising public interest even as a legitimate excuse for breach of rules that restrict access to certain information. As clearly recapped under Article 28 of the Proclamation, even if there exists a law that imposes a limitation on accessing a particular record of information, a public body may not refuse the requested information if the public interest outweighs the protected interest and the harm which would be caused to it as a result of the disclosure.

220. Iterated semantically and with exactly the same narration as it stands in the Constitution, Article 12 of the Press Proclamation recognises the right of everyone to seek, obtain and communicate any information held by public bodies. Including the right to know whether or not the concerned public body is in possession of the entreated information, the person is entitled to have access to and obtain the information by any means appropriate according to the nature of the material. Fittingly, accessing the material may entail inspecting, taking extracts and notes, photocopying the records, copying in diskettes, floppies or any other electronic mode, or printing the desired information from the concerned public authority.

221. Furthermore, perhaps as an impeccable and proactive mechanism in fostering less bureaucratic, prompt, and reasonable setup which guarantees effective and efficient responses to demands of access to public information, the Proclamation under Article 13 has imposed a duty on every public body to publish and make accessible certain information regarding various aspects of the authority. Among other things, updated information such as its duties and responsibilities and the type of the service it offers to the public; its organisational structure and the name and address of the responsible public officer who is in charge of handling requests for information; the available complaint handling mechanisms within the organisation; a brief description as to the type and content of the records available under its disposal and the procedures to be followed while pursuing the materials; the governing rules, regulations, directives, and other guidelines, as well as further particulars regarding its overall function must be advertised to the public.

222. Most crucial is the public body's duty to timely publish all relevant facts concerning important decisions and policies that may affect the public. These include disclosure of the reasons for its decisions alongside dissenting opinions if any – regardless of the nature of the decision being administrative, judicial or quasi-judicial – so that any interested person may have access to inspect and/or receive a copy of the decisions. As it bolsters the culture of transparency and accountability, the authority is also duty bound to publish and communicate the relevant facts to the public in general or to the specific group who will be affected or are likely to be affected about any project, before it enters into effect.

223. Generally, with a concurrent reading of Articles 12 and 13, it can be submitted that the Ethiopian Press Proclamation embodies the right of access to public information in twofold perspectives. On the one hand, it explicitly defines the holders of the right, its content, and the means that may be used as modalities of exercising the right. On the other hand, it delineates the corresponding duty bearer and the substantial matters about the functioning of a public body that need to be published *a priori,* regardless of whether or not a formal request for the information is lodged. In this regard, the enjoyment of the right as enshrined under Article 12 is further reinforced by the subsequent duty imposed on any public body as set forth under Article 13 of the Proclamation. This being the principle regarding the scope of the legal protection to the right, the non-absolute nature of the right of access to information means it becomes subject to certain limitations the application of which would result in some legitimate intrusions justified by the grounds as for explicitly provided under the Proclamation.

224. When it comes to restrictions on the person's freedom of access to public information, Articles 15–25 of the Press Proclamation appears to define the genuine standing of the right and its practical application on the ground. Before advancing into the task of examining the grounds listed as legitimate factors justifying restrictions on the right, it is worth of accentuating the principal rule that governs the source and cogency of the restrictions themselves. First and foremost, Article 15(1) of the Proclamation has rescinded any legislation, other than its own pertinent provisions, which proscribes or restricts the disclosure of information. Furthermore, no administrative decision which classifies a record as a confidential information in and of itself can be invoked as a justification to restrict the person's right of access to the information unless otherwise, the decision fits into one of the excepted grounds as provided in part three of the Proclamation. What could be asserted from such a firm stand of the Proclamation is, therefore, the notion that the exceptions stipulated in part three of the Proclamation as legitimate grounds justifying restrictions on the right are exhaustive ones, and hence no other legislative or administrative measure may be implored as a normative excuse in legitimising any infringement to the right. Being cognisant of this exclusive approach, the exceptions can be clustered into three categories and are analysed as follows.

225. Among the exceptional grounds justifying restrictions on freedom of access to information, the protection to the interest of a third party is postulated as one overriding factor. The two striking issues relevant in the proper application of this exemption would be the question of who is a third party as the holder of the overriding interest, and which types of vested interests are to be protected from disclosure?

226. In regards to the identity of the third party whose interest is prioritised for protection, Article 2(9) of the Proclamation defines the term referring any person other than the person who requested the information (the supplicant) and the public body which is approached to provide the desired information. Hence, a third party could be either an individual private person or other private or public entity having its own legal personality, which also includes a foreign government, either local or international organisation, or an organ of that government or organisation.

227. As to the scope of the protected interest and its administration, Articles 16–19 of the Press Proclamation are presented as the normative basis in dealing with the matter. As a point of departure, Article 16(1) describes the general information relating to a third party as a record of a public body the disclosure of which would involve unreasonable revelation of a personal information about the person. That includes information regarding a deceased person who is yet to be twenty years since his death. Under these circumstances, in principle, the public officer may cast-off the claimant's demand to access the information. Even in such cases, the public relations officer may not reject the request for accessing the record if the third party has not protested against its disclosure, or has expressly consented to endorse the disclosure to the person who has made the request. Furthermore, if the record relates to information that was submitted to the concerned public body by the third party himself, its disclosure cannot be rejected by the public officer as long as the third party was communicated by the time he/she submitted the information in regards to the possibility for its disclosure.

228. In addition, if the information had been already publicised before, rejecting requests for accessing it would be nonsensical. Apart from that, the exclusionary rule is not applicable against a requester who serves as either guardian or tutor of an underage or incapacitated third party individual, given that granting access to the information serves to the latter's best interests. Similarly, access to information about the deceased cannot be rejected if the supplicant is proved to be the deceased's next of kin, or if he/she secures a written consent from the deceased's next of kin in support of his/her request for access to the information. The same is true in regards to access to different work related information about an individual who is or had been an employee of a public body which may include his/her position or status and the responsibilities of the position, title and the services performed, work address, as well as the name as indicated in his/her record. Generally, in full consideration of the rule as it stands under Article 16 of the Press Proclamation, the scope of the restriction on access to information on the ground of protecting the personal information of a third party appears more of as an extra regulatory framework against unnecessary restrictions on the freedom of access to information.

229. The special interest protected under Article 17 of the Proclamation is somewhat different as it aims to maintain safeguards to business secrecy, intellectual property rights, financial confidentialities, and related welfares of a third party. Accordingly, requests demanding access to trade secrets of a third party; to the financial, commercial, scientific, or technical information the disclosure of which is likely to cause damage to his/her commercial or financial interests; as well as to the confidentially supplied information by the third party which may – if disclosed – jeopardise his/her bargaining positions in contractual or other negotiations could be rejected by the public officer according to the circumstances of each case.

230. Notwithstanding such a rule, no refusal to access any of these pieces of information, once they have been made publicly available, may be justified by the rule. Similarly, the absence of any objection against the disclosure of such records by the concerned third party, or his/her express affirmatory consent backing the disclosure would suffice to rebut any measure of restriction. On top of that, the more commanding status of public interest and public safety may override in compelling the disclosure of the aforementioned commercial interests of a third party particularly in circumstances where the disclosure of results of any product or environmental testing or any other investigation or its result supplied by a third party reveals a serious public safety or environmental risk. Here again, as is the case with Article 16, constraining access to information on the ground of protecting the commercial interest of a third party is not an unqualified justification as it remains subject to other considerations that may freeze its application.

231. The third aspect of restriction on the freedom of access to information in lieu of protecting the interest of a third party relates to an information, of which retaining its confidentiality is regarded as a legal or contractual obligation of the individual. As plainly stipulated under Article 18 of the Proclamation, if the disclosure of the information is likely to trigger a legal action against a third party who is under duty to keep the information confidential, access to such a record may be rebuffed by a public officer. Moreover, at times maintaining the continuing flow of confidential information from the third party may necessitate keeping the requested information confidential if its disclosure is likely to prejudice the future supply of similar information on matters involving public interest. In contexts such as these, a public officer may refuse to avail the requested information unless the third party has consented in writing favouring the disclosure of the record to the supplicant who made the request.

232. A thorough reading of Articles 16(2(a & e)), 17(2(b)), and 18(2) of the Proclamation would divulge the special emphasis given to securing the consent of the concerned third party as a crucial leeway in pursuing access to the exceptionally restricted information relating to the person. This entails the public officer to communicate and notify the concerned third party in regards to the intended plan of disclosing the requested record so that he/she may reflect his/her position on the matter within fifteen days after receiving the notice. In so doing, Article 19 of the Proclamation provides an extra guarantee to the individual whose interest is protected under the above cited restrictive provisions of the Proclamation to actively involved in the administration of disclosing the requested information.

233. The second restrictive ground that may legitimately be invoked against the full enjoyment of freedom of access to information relates to the protection to the safety of individuals and of property. Article 20 of the Press Proclamation dictates this justification by authorising the public relations officer of the public body to reject the request for access to information the disclosure of which is found likely to endanger the life or physical safety of an individual. In the same vein, if the disclosure is reasonably presumed to have the impact in prejudicing or impairing methods, plans or procedures for the safety of the public, or any part of the public or for the protection of an individual privileged under the witness protection scheme,[50] blocking access to the requested information may legally be justifiable. Article 20 extends the protection not only to the public or individual's safety but also to certain properties the damage to which is likely to endanger the life or safety of human beings. This category includes information relating to the security of buildings, means of transport, or any other property structure or system – including computer communication system – the disclosure of which would reasonably be expected to prejudice and impair the required safety in the utilisation of these properties.

234. Notwithstanding the conceivable aim, one may logically attach to the nature of the restriction as for provided under Article 20, the very general and 'whole-catching' formulation of its content, however, would invite some excessive and abusive application of the provision in dealing with specific matters on the ground. Given the prohibitive nature of the provision, the conventional rule which demands a narrower interpretation of restrictive provisions and the general prohibition of ascertaining an obligation by analogy should be strictly implemented if Article 20 of the Proclamation is supposed to cover only genuine circumstances that are worth to justify the restriction.

50. Regarding the normative administration of the witness protection scheme, *see* FDRE House of Peoples Representatives, *A Proclamation to Provide for the Protection of Witnesses and Whistle-blowers of Criminal Offences*, Proclamation No. 699/2010, Federal Negarit Gazeta, 17th Year, No. 16 (Addis Ababa 11 Feb. 2011).

§2. Court Hearings and Documents

235. The need to protect information pertaining to judicial and investigative proceedings is the other aspect implored in the Proclamation as one of the *raison d'êtres* that may justify a restriction on access to information. The aim here is more of ensuring confidentiality of information the disclosure of which would otherwise result in prejudicing the effectiveness of the methods, techniques, procedures or guidelines either by leading to the circumvention of the law or in facilitating the commission of an offence. Accordingly, the public relations officer may either refuse to confirm the existence (or otherwise) of the requested information or refuse to block any access to the record if it contains methods, techniques, procedures or guidelines for the prevention, detection, curtailment, or investigation of a contravention of the law, or the prosecution of alleged perpetrators.

236. More specifically on matters relating to prosecution of suspected criminals, Article 21(2) of the Press Proclamation has further entitled the public relations officer to reject requests for access to information about an individual whose prosecution is either under preparation, completed but not instituted, or is pending, if the disclosure is likely to obstruct prosecution. By the same token, the potential fear of a failure of justice or a conceivable impact in eliminating the fairness or impartiality of the trial may also justify rejections for access to the requested information. In a similar fashion, Article 22 of the Proclamation also protects non-disclosure of records containing information which is privileged from production in legal proceedings.

237. In view of the restrictions justified under Articles 21 and 22 of the Proclamation, one may question whether the measures to be taken under the guise of maintaining these objectives are likely to massively endanger the practical observance of the various procedural and evidence-related rights that the suspect is entitled throughout the investigative and trial proceedings. Most decisively, the suspect's right to be informed of the reasons for his/her arrest, the right to have access to all the evidences brought against, in order for him/her to defend his/her case; as well as the right to public trial, and the conventionally demanded standards of transparency in ordinary law enforcement and investigative are highly prone to remain unwarrantedly subjected to these provisions. In this regard, Articles 21 and 22 of the Proclamation are short of precisely delimiting the scope of their application. Perhaps the only exception to rebut such an assertion would be the clause provided under Article 21(3) which excludes the right of access to records that contain information about the general condition of detention of persons held in custody out of the scope of the restriction.

238. Generally, these limitation clauses should in no way be implemented in a manner tarnishing the fundamental substantial and procedural rights that any suspect is entitled at any stage of the investigation and the criminal litigation. The need to make a striking balance between the desired goal of minimising criminal culpability through confidentially conducted expository measures and the ultimate constitutional safeguard against ill-founded prosecutions and convictions will necessitate ensuring the suspect's access to the relevant information that may heighten his/her evidential affluence in the pursuit of defending the case.

239. Perhaps the most controversial and hardly manageable to monitor its practical application is the notion of restricting access to information on the grounds of ensuring the secrecy of military, security and diplomatic operations, that are largely regulated under the highest threshold of confidentiality. Such a strictest standard of clandestineness in their functioning appears to have become the de facto rule to the extent of conceding the perception that information relating to these issues are untouchable businesses of authorities and hence outside of the general public discourse.

240. As is the case in most legal systems – albeit differences as to the degree of the protection and the procedural approaches while regulating its enforcement – the Ethiopian Press Proclamation is not an exception in its contemplation of the aforesaid discernment. To this end, Article 23 of the Proclamation cements the highest standard of confidentiality when it comes to the question of access to information or a request to confirm the (non)existence of a certain information the disclosure of which is believed to cause prejudice to the security, defence and international relation interests of the country. Hence, ascertaining the likelihood of such an impact of making these records accessible would entitle the public relations officer to reject any request to that effect.

241. The most crucial concern pertaining to Article 23 is the scope and non-exhaustive character of the provision in its description of the information to be contained under this category. As mere illustrative lists, information relating to the military operation, exercise, tactics, strategies undertaken in preparation of hostilities, or in connection to the detection, prevention, suppression or curtailment of subversive or hostile activities are designated as records that cannot be obtained. In light of the broader and rather illusively formulated definition ascribed to the conduct of 'subversive or hostile activities' as for provided under Article 2(10) of the Proclamation, such a 'catch-all' submersion of every information under the bigger pot of confidentiality would seriously pose the danger of legitimising and hiding illegal and arbitrary military, intelligence, and at times, even ordinary police operations.

242. Generally, the lists of other information protected under Article 23(2) of the Proclamation can be summarised and reproduced in what follows:

(i) information relating to the quantity, characteristics, capacity, power, vulnerabilities or function or capability or deployment or utility of weapons or any other equipment used for the detecting, preventing or suppressing or curtailing of subversive or hostile activities or anything being designed, developed, produced or considered for use as weapons or such other equipment;

(ii) records about the characteristics, capabilities vulnerability, potential, deployment or function of any military force, unit or personnel or anybody or person entrusted with the task of detecting, preventing, suppressing or curtailing hostile or subversive activities or;

(iii) information held for the purpose of intelligence relating to the national defence or relating to the detection, defence, suppression or curtailment of subversive or hostile activities or relating to another state or an international organisation or used by or on behalf of the country in the process of deliberation and consultation in the conduct of international affairs, and records on the identity of a confidential source and any other source of these information;

(iv) information which is required to be held in confidence by an international agreement or international customary law;

(v) information regarding positions adopted or to be adopted by the country, another state or an international organisation for the purpose of present or future international negotiations;

(vi) information that constitutes diplomatic correspondence exchanged with another state or with an international organisation or official correspondence exchanged with diplomatic missions or consular posts of the country;

(vii) information supplied by or on behalf of the country to another state or an international organisation in terms of an international agreement or arrangement with that state or organisation which requires the information to be held in confidence; and also includes

(viii) all methods of, and scientific or technical equipment for, collecting, assessing or handling the information referred above.

243. A methodical reading of the list would lead one to be sceptical of the unwarrantedly unfastened scope the information exempted from disclosure. Considering the non-exhaustive content of the provision, it seems hardly possible to assume a scenario of securing access to information relating to defence, security, or international relation of the country, which may not be typified as confidential by rescinding the rule as for provided under Article 23. In a country whereby it is not uncommon for the military and the intelligence to routinely engage in ordinary criminal law enforcement missions – rather than sticking to the conventionally known duties and responsibilities of a national defence force – adopting a confidentiality rule with such wide range of application would undoubtedly put not only the constitutional right of access to information in limbo, but also many other rights of the person the violation of which are likely to remain unexposed.

244. Articles 24 and 26 of the Press Proclamation – as the other most disputed contents of the legislation – incorporate seemingly the demand for ensuring administrative secrecy in the operation of public bodies. Highly criticised as a normative leeway in obliterating press freedom by shrouding the works of government in a despicable secrecy, Article 24 empowers the public relations officer to reject any request for Cabinet documents, or to refuse to confirm the existence or otherwise non-existence of information contained in a cabinet record in so far as it is not made available to the public by the decision of the Cabinet.

245. In comparison to the restrictive clauses discussed so far, Article 24 appears stickier and nonsensical given that it does not even theoretically indicate the rationale behind the restriction and the specific interest to be protected, or the nature and type of the damage to be prevented by maintaining the secrecy of these documents. What is more difficult to comprehend is the absolute discretion given to the Cabinet in deciding the type information to be public and the one to be kept confidential. In light of such a mandate fully vested in the hands of the executive political powerhouse called the Cabinet – coupled with the very wide range of documents classified as Cabinet documents pursuant to the lists as for provided under Article 24(2), a list which is not exhaustive in itself – the constitutional demand for transparency and accountability in the conduct of affairs of the government does not seem to have the necessary legislative backup that may rescind the risk posed by Article 24 against the freedom of access to public information.

246. The same unavoidable risk holds true with regards to the nature of the information exempted from disclosure as per Article 26 of the Proclamation. Here again, without stipulating the intended interest to be protected or the purpose that necessitated the restriction, the public relations officer is authorised to refuse any request for access to records of the public body if:

> the record contains an opinion, advice, report or recommendation obtained or prepared or an account of a consultation, discussion or deliberation that has occurred, including, but not limited to, minutes of a meeting, for the purpose of assisting to formulate a policy or take a decision in the exercise of a power or performance of a duty conferred or imposed by law.

Looking at the content of matters covered under the restriction clause, it cannot be disputed that the stated activities are ought to be the traditional functions of any public body depending on the specific duties and responsibilities assigned to it as per the establishing law. Accordingly, rejecting access to the information that is so connected to its inherent task would result in nothing but a granting a flawed and unfortified normative backup to the undesirable culture of secrecy in the everyday institutional performance of the public body in question.

247. The remaining lists as for provided under the remaining paragraphs of Article 26 have also little – if not nothing – to offer in rectifying and remedying the potential abuses in the interpretation and practical application of the provision. In this regard, sub-paragraph (b) of Article 26(1), for example, resembles to forestall the need to keep confidentiality of records merely on the fear of potential frustration of deliberative processes in the public body or among the public bodies if the record is to be made public. Instead of entrenching the institutional culture of candid communication of opinion, advice, recommendations, discussions, deliberations, or consultation conducts within and among public bodies, setting secrecy as the rule of the game appears to reflect the puzzle surrounding Proclamation's superfluous approach. Furthermore, paragraph 2 of Article 26 has expanded the public relation officer's power of blocking access to information upon suspicions that its disclosure may jeopardise the public body's effectiveness in monitoring, auditing, testing or examining through its procedures or methods. Similarly, a record that contains evaluative material may also be kept confidential, if the disclosure of which is likely to breach an express or implied promise made to that effect. A legally binding agreement of non-disclosure or even an expressly declared promise is not a requirement as the promise could also be impliedly ascertained upon the discretion of the public relations officer in the course of entertaining the request.

248. Generally, as it stands, the exemptions stipulated under Articles 24 and 26 and their impact in impending access to information under the government's possession serves no justifiable purpose other than exacerbating the long-standing problem of the culture of secrecy in government operation.

249. Last but not least – and arguably, in what appears to be at odds to the highly demanded notion of transparent and uncorrupted involvement of public bodies in dealing with the economic and financial interests of the country – Article 25 of the Proclamation presents the rule of confidentiality as a protective mechanism of the public body's economic and commercial interest, and hence, as a justifiable ground in objurgating any request for its disclosure. Accordingly, the public relation officer may refuse to grant access to the requested record of information if its release is presumed 'to jeopardise the economic interests or financial welfare of the nation, or the ability of the government to manage the economy of the country'. Cemented in detail with a non-exhaustive list of records to be covered under the exemption, this provision also represents the marked shortcomings of the Proclamation in jolting the requirement of precision and lucidity of intrusive provisions against the freedom of access to public information.

250. In what may be described as an attempt to monitor the practical implementation of the restrictive provisions discussed so far, Articles 28, 29, and 39 of the Proclamation have set certain priorities that should in no way be conflated under the guise of enforcing the law. The first guiding rule in this aspect is the supremacy of public interest. In view of this value, whenever there exists conflict between the aim of protecting certain interest as per the exemption clauses (Articles 15–25) and the public interest that necessitates disclosure, the public relation officer may not refuse access to the requested information unless the harm to be caused to the protected interest following the disclosure outweighs the public interest.

251. Apart from that, the fact that a certain document contains partially confidential or protected information does not warrant a complete rejection of access to the entire document. As long as the record can be sifted and separated without causing damage to the protected interest, the rest component of the record has to be made accessible to the requester. Even the protection given to confidential information is not absolute. As plainly stated under Article 39(2) of the Proclamation, no one should be subjected to legal, employment or administrative-related sanctions for disclosing information on wrongdoing; or other information the disclosure of which would expose a serious threat to health and the safety of the environment. In so doing, no one shall be responsible for any breach of legal or contractual obligation as long as he/she acts in good faith with a reasonable belief as to the substantial truthfulness of the information while disclosing these potential harms to the public. Most notably, Article 39(3) specifically outlaws accountability for any act of exposing the commission of a criminal offence; disclosing failure to comply with the legal obligation, uncovering miscarriage of justice, corruption, or dishonesty, or revealing abuse of power or serious misconduct. Hence, on matters relating to these happenings, no legal or contractual obligation can be invoked as a justifying ground to abstain from disclosing the relevant information. Article 39(6) further strengthens such a position by prohibiting any act of making any document confidential aiming to cover corruption, contravention of the law, to camouflage organisational or personal incompetence, inefficiency or scandals.

252. Concerning the ethical and administrative conducts of a person in his/her capacity as the public relations officer, Article 39 of the Proclamation provides the general presumption, prohibited grounds for non-disclosure, and the liabilities that may arise upon infringing the duties in the course of exercising his/her mandate. Accordingly, as a rule, no public relations officer or any other person may be criminally or civilly held accountable for any action or inaction made in good faith while exercising his/her mandate in the course of implementing the provisions that regulate the person's right to access to public information. This said, any deliberate denial of a right of access to information by either destroying, damaging, altering, concealing, or falsifying of a record, would, however, amount as a punishable offence with potential fine or imprisonment for up to two years up on conviction. In light of this, the purpose under Article 39(4) could best be ascribed as a normative safeguard against any abusive conduct under the guise of exercising the power of administering the person's right to access to public information vis-à-vis an opposite application of some restrictive measures based on the legitimate grounds as for explicitly provided in the Proclamation.

253. The fact that the requested information is not among those legally exempted from disclosure may not automatically guarantee the supplicant's actual and straight access to the record. Even in the pursuit of information legally deemed accessible, the law may still require the applicant to observe certain procedures and formalities, of which a failure to comply may result in delay or at times even total rejection of the request. Hence, if any prospect for a genuine enforcement of the right of access to public information is to become a reality, not only should the restrictive provisions be exhaustive and narrowly interpreted, the law shall also establish a system that accommodates requests with simple, flexible, inexpensive, and easily reachable procedures and technical formalities.

254. Needless to say, access to fresh and actual information is perhaps the one, and at times, the only vein that gives life to the work of the press and its survival in the media market. The more the information disclosure procedure is stranded by extremely stretched hierarchical channels, unnecessary formalities, and bureaucratic hindrances, the higher would the danger of imperilling the inherent function of media and journalists in fulfilling their duty of informing the public and shaping public discourses on matters involving its interest. Accordingly, the value of the pertinent provisions of the law which govern the procedural and technical aspects in the administration of the right should be sensitised as equally important as the substantive provisions that give rise to the recognition of the right and their normative significance in defining its content and scope of application.

255. Having these general remarks in mind, what comes next as a point of discussion is the issue of whether the Ethiopian Press Proclamation contains the required normative procedural and formality guidelines aimed at regulating the enforcement of the right in a manner that ensures judicious, expeditious, and inexpensive access to the requested information. In this regard, Articles 13, 14, 19 and 27 of the Proclamation are the provisions one may have to consult in responding to various issues pertaining to procedure, time and matters of formality.

256. To begin with, Article 13 imposes a self-standing obligation on a public body to publish information relating – among other things – to all its organisational structure; functional duties and responsibilities; administrative hierarchies and their official duties and mandates; the directives, regulations, guidelines, and manuals which govern the activities and functions of its various organs and the employees; the intra-grievance handling and dispute settlement mechanisms; as well as a brief catalogue and description of information under its disposal together with a description of the procedures to be followed in the course of requesting for access to such records. The significance of Article 13 can be seen in twofold perspectives. One the one hand, the duty to publish is set as a proactive duty that should not be contingent upon responding to particular requests for accessing the information. On the other hand, the more the desired information is prepared and made available in advance, the higher the prospect becomes of securing the requested record as promptly as the press demands.

257. Once a person opts to exercise his/her right of accessing a certain public information, questions such as what exactly to ask; whom to communicate; under which communication modality; when to submit the request; and the reasonable time it takes to receive the entreated matter will have to be addressed in light of the specific normative standards prescribed by the law. As it stands, Article 14 of the Press Proclamation contemplates to resolve most of these procedural and formality issues.

258. In regards to the content to be requested, the applicant is expected to clearly identify what he/she is looking for, and present same to the responsible public relations officer of the public body in question. Reading Article 14 in conjunction with Article 27 of the Proclamation, failure to provide a request for a specific and clearly defined information may result in refusal of access to the record. Quite uncomfortably, Article 27 authorises the public relation officer to reject any request to obtain information if the demand is deemed 'too general', insufficiently precise, or is of the nature that the task of retrieving or processing it would require to involve disproportionate diversion of human and material resources to the extent which may adversely affect the routine functioning of the public body. This being the rule, even if the applicant may exert a candid effort to minimise potential rejections through a proper narration of his/her clear demands, its application is still left in the hands of the officer who is entitled to determine on each case according to circumstances. Trickier as it appears, justifying rejections for access to information relying merely on the public officer's impression as to the impression or generality of the request would serve no objective other than exposing the system to remain patchy and unpredictable. For that matter, the possibility of cases in which the applicant may not be in a position to determine the nature and specific content of the desired information cannot be ruled out, and hence, the requisite of precision should not be invoked to preclude demands to obtain information of such a kind. In view of this, the applicant should have at least had a second chance of briefing the content of the request before granting the officer with unwarranted power to reject it.

259. Most importantly, as clearly noted under Article 14(2), apart from the general expectation of clarity and precision in setting the requested information, the applicant is not required to provide any reason why he/she is pursuing to obtain the information. The other issue relates to the modality of presenting the request. Normally, any request to obtain a certain information should be communicated in writing or through electronic devices, such as via emails or fax. Indeed, if the requester is found to be illiterate or physically disable to fulfil the requirement of the written submission, the public officer is duty bound to provide assistance in providing a written request in the prescribed form.

260. Once the applicant communicated the request to the public relations officer, the latter is duty bound to respond as expeditiously as possible, either by providing the requested information or with a written notice of the rejection by clearly stating the reasons thereof. The question here is the time threshold in defining promptness. Article 14(3) provides a period of one month as of the formal submission of the request as a standard, of which for all the possible reasons, does not seem to match the reasonably required time framework. More awkwardly, the public officer also holds the discretion to extend such a deadline for additional thirty working days upon the circumstances as for provided under Article 14(8).

261. Only in exceptional circumstances where the request relates to access to information on a matter which is deemed urgent, Article 14(9) reduces the period to ten working days within which the public relations officer shall provide the requested information. Promisingly, even paragraph 'b' of Article 14(10) tends to categorise the task of requesting information for the purpose of journalistic work – i.e., dissemination of information in the mass media – under the domain of requests which may demand an urgent response. However, even setting aside the question of whether a ten-day period itself is prompt enough in light of what a reasonably urgent matter would normally entail a swift reply, the prospect for proper implementation of the provision remains unsettled mainly because the public relations officer still holds the power to determine whether a certain matter is urgent or not; a decision which, pursuant to Article 14(11) of the Proclamation, is not subject to judicial appeal other than lodging petition for a review of the decision through the organisation's internal administration. This judicially untouchable discretion of the public body in deciding on matters of urgency would effectually make the ten-day minimum period practically inconsequential.

262. The prolongation of the time becomes even poorer if the officer rejects the request; a decision that may have to be challenged through appeal procedure which requires further time and labour of its own. Furthermore, Article 14(5) has by default invalidated the requirement of giving a written notice of refusal within one month after receiving the request, given that it allows implied rejection simply by failing to respond after the expiry of the period. Such an implied rejection obliterates not only the person's right to receive an informed response about the request but also his/her right to appeal against the decision as there is no way to learn the reasons invoked in justifying the refusal.

263. Generally, in full consideration of these inconsistently stipulated time standards, the issue of promptness does not seem to hold the required normative backup as it stands in the Proclamation. This relaxed approach, which thwarts the freedom of access to information under the shadow of the bureaucrat's prerogative gravely endangers the public's right to know of matters of public interest as promptly as possible.

264. Basically, the public relation's decision of rejecting requests for access to information is not final, and hence, it is appealable. As governed under the provisions from Articles 31 to 34 of the Press Proclamation, depending on the content and the stages or phases it has to go through, appeals can be divided into three: intra-organisational appeal, administrative appeal, and then judicial appeal. Indeed, not every case can be taken to the court through appeal – as some decisions, such as a decision as highlighted above, on urgency or otherwise of a certain request pursuant to Article 14(11) – any action of appeal would require first to assess the nature of the issue whether it is appealable or not.

265. As a starting point, once the public relations officer notifies the rejection of the request to obtain information, any applicant aggrieved by such a decision may institute his/her appeal to the concerned head of the public body. Such an intra-organisational appeal has to be communicated within thirteen days after the initial decision was made by the public officer. As briefly noted, the public officer may impliedly reject a request without expressly responding to it as inaction within one month after receiving the application is deemed as a refusal. The challenge here is, unless the supplicant is unambiguously informed of the reasons for the refusal, his/her appeal will have no substantial content other than blindly petitioning regarding the unexplained denial of the right to access and obtain the requested information. Implied rejection would also make it difficult to exactly determine the period of limitation within which the aggrieved applicant is ought to exercise his/her appeal right. From these standpoints, allowing implied rejection infringes not only the applicant's right to be informed of expressly reasoned decisions, it also throws their right to appeal in limbo, challenging the substantial aspects of the decision within the time specified in the Proclamation. Be that as it may, once the applicant succeeds in lodging his/her appeal to the concerned head of the public body in question, the latter has to address the case and give a decision within ten days after receiving the complaint.

266. If the applicant still remains discontented with the decision after exhausting the intra-organisational complaint handling mechanism, he/she may institute the proper administrative appeal to the specifically entrusted body called the Ombudsman; an Institution established pursuant to Proclamation No. 211/2001. Timewise, as for provided under Articles 31(4) and 33 of the Proclamation, appeal to the Ombudsman has to be lodged within a month after receiving the decision rendered by the head of the concerned public body. While dealing with such a particular mandate, the office of Ombudsman may inspect records held by the public body that are relevant in reviewing the case. This being the rule, the Office may be restricted of consulting records classified as confidential as per Article 35, and those exempted from disclosure pursuant to the specific provisions of the Proclamation discussed hitherto.

267. As a final outcome of its review, the Ombudsman may either reject the appeal or instruct the public body to provide the requested information or take any other measure aimed at ensuring the public body's commitment in implementing its obligations as envisaged under the Proclamation. Whatever it may be, the Ombudsman has to make a judgment on the matter and announce its verdict within a month after receiving the appeal.

268. It is then after the Ombudsman's decision that the aggrieved party may further resort to judicial appeal as a final adjudicatory platform where the case becomes the subject of ordinary court review. Accordingly, a judicial appeal has to be submitted within thirty days after learning of the Ombudsman's decision either to the Federal First Instance Court – if the matter related to a federal public body – or to the opposite Regional High Court, in case if the party involved is a regional public body. What seems unclear at this juncture is the status of whether the decision of the Federal First Instance or the Regional High Court – depending on the case – should be regarded as final or should still be subject to the appellate jurisdiction of higher courts. Given that explicit indication as to the finality of the decision is cemented nowhere in the Proclamation, any assertion to that effect may lead to disregarding the person's right of appeal, at least on issues of law if not on matters of fact. On the other, granting such uncharted and extended strings of appeal may unnecessarily prolong the procedure, the time, and cost to the extent proving counterproductive to the press's right of prompt and inexpensive access to obtain information, and to the public's general right to know, of the public information as expeditiously as possible.

269. Throughout its substantial task in the course of reviewing the case, the court may examine any record of the public body. Accordingly, other than those explicitly classified as confidential pursuant to Article 35 and information exempted from disclosure as per the pertinent provisions of the Proclamation, no record of the public body can be reserved out of the court's spectacle on any ground. At times, if maintaining the confidentiality of the information if believed necessary, the court may receive evidence or hear arguments in the absence of either the applicant or his/her representative. Whatever may be deemed appropriate in terms of procedure, the court shall render judgment on the case, including on issues of payments or expenses, within thirty days as of the day of appeal.

Chapter 6. Press Council

270. There is no legislative framework for the establishment, function and operation of the press council in Ethiopia. However, there is an ongoing discussion for the establishment of a press council in Ethiopia.

Part III. Regulation of Audiovisual Media (Broadcasting)

271. Broadcasting media is a late twentieth century phenomenon in Ethiopia. Radio broadcasting was introduced to Ethiopia in 1935, while television broadcasting started in 1963 by transmitting the first meetings of the Organisation of African Unity (now African Union). Broadcasting service in Ethiopia has been heavily state controlled. As a result, the broadcasting media operation mirrors the political and ideological leanings of the government of the time. During the imperial regime, the Ethiopian Radio and Television Agency transmitted news, information, entertainment and educational programmes promoting the good images of the Emperor and his good government. To this effect, a censorship board was established under the Press and Information Office in the Ministry of Pen.[51] The broadcasting of news and programmes had to undergo pre-censorship by the board. Similarly, in the military regime, the Ethiopian Radio and Television Agency was a socialist and communist propaganda machine. By the same token, public broadcasting service during the current regime is a medium of disseminating its own ideologies, programmes, policies, and preferences.

272. While the *modus operandi* of public service broadcasting during the imperial, *Derg,* and EPRDF regimes is the same, there is a relatively diverse and plural broadcasting service in EPRDF's Ethiopia. Not only is there a private broadcasting service in Ethiopia, there is also a decentralised media landscape. Despite their limitations in coverage both of space and issues, there are private radio and television broadcasting services in Ethiopia today. Further, as the country follows a federal system, there are public service broadcasting services at the regional level. The Ethiopian Broadcasting Corporation (EBC), the previous Ethiopian Radio and Television Agency, is the public broadcasting service of the federal government. The nine regional states and the City Administrations of Addis Ababa and Dire Dawa have their own Radio and Television broadcasting services. Hence, Ethiopia has thirteen public broadcasting services with their own legal, institutional and programme choices.

51. Terje S. Skjerdal, *Competing Loyalties: Journalism Culture in the Ethiopian State Media*, Ph.d. thesis, 11–12 (University of Bergen 2012).

273. In addition to the decentralisation of the broadcasting media landscape, there are three types of broadcasting services. These are the public broadcasting service, the commercial broadcasting service and the community broadcasting service.[52] These broadcasting services can be transmitted at the national, regional or local levels. While the national transmission covers a broadcasting service more than one region, the regional transmission is limited to broadcasting to one region, and the local transmission is limited to one *Wereda* or municipality.[53]

52. FDRE House of Peoples Representatives, *Proclamation No. 533/2007 Broadcasting Service Proclamation*, Federal Negarit Gazeta, 13th Year No. 39 (ADDIS ABABA, 23 Jul. 2007), Arts 2(9), 10 & 11.
53. *Ibid.*, Arts 2(15), (16) & (17).

Chapter 1. Public Service Broadcasting

§1. The Concept and Mission of Public Service Broadcasting

274. Broadcasting services in Ethiopia are highly related to the development ambition of the state. As such, a broadcasting service is considered as instrumental to the socio-economic and political development of the country by providing information and educating the public. It is no wonder that the government has controlled the broadcasting service in a monopoly for much of its operation. A cursory reading of the numerous legislation on broadcasting service in Ethiopia reveals that broadcasting services are a means for development and transformation of the country and its people. While a reference to freedom of expression and information is mentioned in this legislation, the chief rationale and purpose of broadcasting services is their significant role in the development of the country. For instance, the Ethiopian Broadcasting Proclamation in its preamble provides the twofold rationale for broadcasting service. In its opening paragraph, it states that 'broadcasting services play a significant role in the political, economic and social development of the country by providing information, education and entertainment programmes to the public'.[54] This is followed by the affirmation of the major role broadcasting services play in 'exercising the basic constitutional rights such as freedom of expression, access to information and the right to elect and be elected'.[55] The order in which these rationales are provided is not without ramifications. As it is evident in practice, the developmental role of broadcasting services trumps its rights enforcement. Put differently, broadcasting services as a channel of freedom of expression and access to information becomes secondary. This legislative design with the official developmental state ideology of the incumbent regime positions broadcasting services at the service of development communication.[56]

275. The Broadcasting proclamation defines public service broadcasting as a radio or television transmission service established for the purpose of educating, informing, and entertaining the public, in the federal or a regional state to which government budget is allocated in full or in part and is accountable to the federal or regional parliaments.[57] Indeed, public service broadcasting in Ethiopia has a public service feature in the sense that it should advance some public purpose. Accordingly, public service broadcasting in Ethiopia is tasked with five responsibilities.[58] The first is to enhance the participation of the public through the presentation of government policies and strategies as well as activities related to development, democracy and good governance. The second is to present programmes which inform, educate and entertain the public; while the third is to present programmes which reflect the unity of peoples based on equality. The fourth responsibility is to promote and enhance the cultures and artistic values of the public and the final one

54. *Ibid.*, preamble para. 1.
55. *Ibid.*, preamble para. 2.
56. Christopher Clapham, *The Ethiopian Developmental State*, 39 *Third World Quarterly* 1 (2017).
57. Broadcasting proclamation, *supra* note 52, Art. 2(9).
58. *Ibid.*, Art. 16(2).

is to serve lawfully operating political parties on the basis of fair and just treatment. Although each of these responsibilities are interconnected, their specific mention is to emphasise the role of the state and its media in the development and transformation of the country, to recognise the cultural and ethnic diversity of its people, and to build a country, based on the ideals of equality, democracy and unity.

276. The EBC Establishment Proclamation reiterates the concept and mission of public broadcasting services provided in the Broadcasting Service Proclamation. EBC comprises the Ethiopian radio and television broadcasting services. These are the public broadcasting services at the federal or national level. The establishing proclamation of EBC states that EBC is a bridge between the government and the people. The public broadcasting service rendered by EBC is expected to connect the government and the people by ensuring civic participation, promoting the free expression of ideologies and views among society for its common benefit.[59] In terms of legislative design, EBC can be a broadcasting service of diverse views and opinions including of political parties and individuals. EBC has two objectives; the first is to broadcast main and current issues happening in the country and around the world and to broadcast programmes which educate and entertain the public; while the second is to create national consensus, identity, dignity, and democratic unity by respecting diversity and promoting tolerance.[60] EBC is not only expected to be a channel of communication and information, but also an active participant in the development of the country.[61] It assumes an important developmental role as any public institution in the country.

277. In furthering these objectives, EBC has a number of powers and duties. The first is to collect news and news packages which are deemed relevant and important for society.[62] Both what is relevant and important for society and who decides on these matters is crucial for access to information. The paternalistic approach of the law that EBC can collect news and disseminate them on the condition of relevance and importance to society can be abused to exclude some news from broadcasting. The second is to present educational and informative programmes with the objective to mobilise the public for development, good governance, and democratic system.[63] By the same token, what is broadcasted are the kind of programmes which are supposed to mobilise the public towards certain ends. As noted above, this can be used to mainstream a particular set of programmes while ignoring or marginalising others. However, EBC is also mandated to broadcast programmes which create awareness of human and democratic rights and to receive and broadcast free public opinions and disclosures.[64]

---

59. FDRE House of Peoples Representatives, *Proclamation No. 858/2014, Ethiopian Broadcasting Corporation Establishment Proclamation*, Federal Negarit Gazeta (Addis Ababa 20th Year No. 79, 8 Nov. 2014), preamble.
60. *Ibid.*, Art. 5.
61. *Ibid.*, Art. 5(1).
62. *Ibid.*, Art. 6(1).
63. *Ibid.*, Art. 6(2).
64. *Ibid.*, Art. 6(3 & 4).

278. The vision of Ethiopian Radio and Ethiopian Television is to be the most preferable and influential broadcaster in Africa. And its mission is to reaffirm the Ethiopian renaissance.

§2. The Organisation of Public Service Broadcasting

279. The organisation of public service broadcasting in Ethiopia is government controlled. EBC is the organisation responsible for public service broadcasting. Its establishment proclamation expressly states that EBC is an autonomous government institution rendering public service and accountable to the parliament.[65] As such, while it is deemed to be autonomous it is a government institution and responsible to the government of the day. EBC has the following organisational structure. It has a Board, the Chief Executive Office, necessary Deputy Chief Executive Officers, and the necessary staff.[66] Hence, the needs and tasks of EBC will determine how many Deputy Chief Executive Officers and staff it should have to execute its responsibilities and functions.

280. The Board is comprised of a chairperson and seven members are chosen from different pertinent institutions and sections of the society.[67] The idea is that the board should be plural enough to include different interests and voices in the society, which EBC should channel. However, members of the Board are appointed by the House of Peoples' Representatives based on the recommendation of the Prime Minister.[68] Accordingly, the selection and approval of the members of the Board have to pass through a political process. This is due to the fact that the Board has to get the support of the executive and of the parliament for its constitution. This is particularly problematic in a country like Ethiopia where there is an absolute overlap between the executive and the parliament. When such overlap is compounded by a single dominant party system, there is a possibility that the Board will be another wing of the party and the government in the public broadcasting service. Related to this, the term of office of the Board is five years which coincides with the term of office of the parliament.[69] Accordingly, the autonomy of the Board and its role in guiding the public service broadcasting will be contingent upon the political atmosphere of the time. When there is an enabling political atmosphere, the Board can execute its autonomous governmental public function, in the absence of an enabling political atmosphere, the Board cannot ensure its independence and autonomy as a matter of legislative design.

---

65. *Ibid.*, Art. 3.
66. *Ibid.*, Art. 7.
67. *Ibid.*, Art. 8(1).
68. *Ibid.*, Art. 8(3).
69. *Ibid.*, Art. 8(4).

281. Partly related to its establishment and accountability as noted above, the Board's main powers and duties are related to ensuring the communication of government policies and laws in the public service broadcasting efficiently and sufficiently to the society.[70] In addition to this, the Board takes measures to improve the provision of public service broadcasting through programme evaluation and assessment to advance the missions and visions of EBC.[71] The Board has a regular meeting once a month and can hold emergency meetings at the request of one-third of its members.[72] Although the law provides for the appointment and accountability of the Board, it does not provide who and how members of the Board are dismissed. Nonetheless, as they are appointed by the House of Peoples' Representatives with the recommendation of the Prime Ministers, the dismissal process may follow the same procedure.

282. The Chief Executive Officer, the secretary and member of the Board,[73] are appointed by the House of Peoples' Representatives upon recommendation by the Prime Minister.[74] However, the Deputy Chief Executive Officers are appointed by the Board upon recommendation by the Chief Executive Officer.[75] Like members of the Board, the law does not specify grounds for the dismissal of the Chief Executive Officer or her deputies. Like appointment, dismissal is also an important matter that requires legislative regulation. Without a prior legal requirement of dismissal, it becomes difficult and arbitrary to dismiss a Chief Executive Officer or her deputies. This legal gap can harm their personal independence and institutional autonomy by extension.

§3. The Financing of Public Service Broadcasting

283. EBC finances its operation from different sources.[76] The first is from revenues it collects in rendering its services. Although its main function is public service, it is entitled to collect service charges and fees. [77] These include revenues collected from advertisements and sponsored programmes.[78] However, the generation of revenues from advertisements is not unlimited. Unless it is an advertisement station, it is prohibited to broadcast advertisements for more than 20% of both the daily transmission time or within a particular programme time for advertisements.[79] The second source of revenue for EBC is a government funding. The government allocates an annual budget for EBC as it does for any other government institution. And the final one is EBC can collect from other sources. Nonetheless, how and from

70. *Ibid.*, Art. 9(1 & 2).
71. *Ibid.*, Art. 9(3–6).
72. *Ibid.*, Art. 10.
73. *Ibid.*, Art. 8(5).
74. *Ibid.*, Art. 11(1).
75. *Ibid.*, Art. 12(1).
76. *Ibid.*, Art. 14.
77. *Ibid.*, Art. 6(8).
78. Broadcasting service proclamation, *supra* note 52, Arts 33 & 36.
79. *Ibid.*, Art. 35.

whom EBC collects in this regard is not clearly stipulated in the law. For instance, it may collect revenues from donations, gifts, and fundraisings.

Chapter 2. Private Broadcasting

§1. Different Categories of Private Broadcasters

284. Private broadcasting in Ethiopia is referred to as commercial broadcasting. The law regulates the traditional broadcasting service through radio and television. As a result, Internet broadcasting is not included in the category of commercial broadcasting. The broadcasting service proclamation defines commercial broadcasting as 'a radio or television transmission service established for profit by a legal entity with the purpose of informing, educating or entertaining the public'.[80] As it is evident, private broadcasting is limited to radio and television transmission services whose objective is the making of profit while informing, educating and entertaining the public.

285. Private broadcasting can be transmitted at the national, regional or local levels. A national transmission service is a transmission service which covers more than one region, while a regional transmission service is limited to one region, a local transmission service is limited to a municipality or *wereda*.[81] At all levels, a private broadcasting service is required to equally treat the community within its licence area: its programmes should cover the whole area of its licence, and include regional and national news in its programmes.[82]

286. In addition to private broadcasting, there is community broadcasting. Community broadcasting is 'a non-profit radio or television transmission service established by the will and interest of a community and Administered and run by the community living in a specific area or who possess a common interest'.[83] A community broadcasting does not have an obligation to cover regional and national news, unlike the commercial broadcasting. However, any community broadcasting service is mandated to carry out activities in accordance with the specific needs of the community with respect to development, education and good governance. This obligation may require a community broadcasting service to cover regional and national news as these will affect the community.[84] The main emphasis of community broadcasting services is related to the promotion of the participation of the people and enhance its awareness on issues involving the community, the promotion of the culture, language, and artistic expressions of the community, and broadcasting programmes affecting the community that do not get coverage by other broadcasting services.[85]

80. *Ibid.*, Art. 2(10).
81. *Ibid.*, Art. 2 (15–17).
82. *Ibid.*, Art. 16(3).
83. *Ibid.*, Art. 2(11).
84. *Ibid.*, Art. 16(4) (a).
85. *Ibid.*, Art. 16(4) (b–f).

287. Both commercial and community broadcasting services should choose one of the following broadcasting service licenses: terrestrial to air free radio broadcasting service, terrestrial to air free television broadcasting service, satellite radio broadcasting service, satellite television broadcasting service, satellite broadcasting service provided to customers for fee, receiving and broadcasting foreign programmes to customers for fee, cable television broadcasting service provided to customers for fee, and other broadcasting services to be prescribed by the EBA.[86] Hence, the law does not regulate broadcasting services through the Internet nor non-linear broadcasting services. It focuses on the regulation of traditional broadcasting services on radio and television on a linear basis. Further, it does not regulate on demand video services. As it stands now, the market for on demand video services and non-linear services is very limited given the technological development of the country and the demands of its people.

§2. Licensing Requirements

288. Every broadcaster, including public, commercial and community broadcasters, is prohibited to operate without a licence in Ethiopia.[87] There are two ways to get a license for broadcasting. The first is through the invitation of the EBA and the second is an application for a licence at any time. The EBA invites applicants by a notice published in a newspaper or any other mass media having a wider circulation disclosing the category of broadcasting service for which the license is intended to be issued, the licence area, the radio wave available, time and place of submission of application, the license fee and other necessary information.[88] Based on this call, a person can apply for a license for a broadcasting service. In spite of this, public and community broadcasting service license can be asked anytime.[89] As a result, the license for commercial broadcasting service is regulated and should fit with the standards, needs and preferences of the Authority. This makes the license requirements for a commercial broadcasting service cumbersome in Ethiopia.

289. However, not all persons are entitled to have a license for broadcasting. There are a number of conditions that must be met to have a license. The first is related to the financial capacity of the person applying for a license and the second is related to the nature of the person. If the person fails to produce evidence to ascertain its financial capacity and sources of funding or detailed project proposal, the application will be rejected without even detail screening.[90] Similarly, if the person applying for a broadcasting license falls into the category of persons that are not allowed to have a broadcasting service, the application will be rejected.[91] Article 23 of the Broadcasting Service Proclamation lists the categories of persons who are not entitled to have a license for broadcasting. According to this Article, individuals and

86. *Ibid.*, Art. 17.
87. *Ibid.*, Art. 18.
88. *Ibid.*, Art. 19(1) (2).
89. *Ibid.*, Art. 19(4).
90. *Ibid.*, Art. 20(1 & 2).
91. *Ibid.*, Art. 20(3).

persons who are not given a legal personality are not entitled to have a broadcasting license. This means that an individual has to establish an organisation to have a license. Further, an organisation which is not incorporated in Ethiopia and whose capital or management is controlled by foreign nationals are not allowed to have a license. Similarly, a political organisation or where a political organisation is a shareholder or a member of a political organisation's supreme leadership is a shareholder or member of its management at any level or a religious organisation is prohibited from having a broadcasting license. In addition, an organisation of which its owner or any of its owners or a member of its management is convicted of a serious crime or an organisation of which more than 50% of its capital is held by another organisation which carries on the business of printed press or news agency or a person that owns more than 20% of the capital of such organisation are prohibited from a broadcasting business.

290. Article 21 of the broadcasting service proclamation provides the criteria for issuing a license. In making a decision to issue or reject a license, the EBA considers (1) the reliability and sufficiency of the applicant's financial sources to run the service; (2) the applicant's organisational capacity, knowledge and experience to render the service; (3) the contents of the programme submitted by the applicant and social needs covered by the programme, and (4) the transmission time allocated for the service. If the authority rejects the application, it is obligated to give reasons and the applicant has the right to appeal to the Board.[92] The application for appeal has to be made within fourteen days of the decision and the Board shall give its decision within twenty days of receiving the appeal.

291. The validity period of the broadcasting license varies depending on whether it concerns broadcasting at the national, regional or local level or on whether the broadcasting service is radio or television. The license at the local level has the longest duration while at the national level it is short. Also, the duration of a television license is longer than a radio license. A broadcasting license in Addis Ababa has the shortest duration even compared with Dire Dawa. A radio and television transmission service at the national level have eight and ten years license duration respectively, while at the regional level the years increase by two for both radio and television, and at the local level they increase by another two years.[93] A radio and television transmission service license in Dire Dawa has ten and twelve years of duration respectively, while in Addis Ababa it is six and eight years respectively.[94] On the other hand, a community broadcasting service is issued for five years unless it is a short term broadcasting which should not be valid for more than a year.[95] It looks like the broadcasting service at the national level and in Addis Ababa is regulated more as they have the shortest duration. Given the impact of broadcasting at the national level and in Addis Ababa, the government tries to control it more strictly than regional or local broadcasters or those in Dire Dawa.

92. *Ibid.*, Art. 22.
93. *Ibid.*, Art. 24(1–3).
94. *Ibid.*, Art. 24(4 & 5).
95. *Ibid.*, Art. 24(6 & 7).

292. If a broadcaster chooses to expand its services after the license, it has to get an expansion license. As in the original application for the license, broadcasters should convince the EBA on the expansion and utility to the community. Additional broadcasting service, upgrading the capacity of the station or making technological changes and upgrading the capacity of the transmitter or request for a new radio wave to cover other areas outside of its license area require an expansion license.[96] In addition, renewal of license is possible and an application for renewal has to be made not sooner than one year and not later than six months before the expiry of the license.[97] In renewing the license, the main consideration is the acceptability of the broadcasting service by the community and the satisfaction of the community to the broadcasting service. If there are repeated records of complaints by the community against the broadcasting service, the authority may decline renewing the license. However, how many complaints constitute repeated complaints are not clear and the ultimate decision rests in the discretionary power of the authority that renews the license. Unlike the original license, the duration of the renewed license is determined by the authority and there is no fixed period.[98]

293. Nonetheless, the license may be suspended and revoked before the expiry of its period. The license may be suspended when the broadcaster violates any of the provisions of the Broadcasting Service Proclamation. However, the broadcaster is entitled to appeal its grievances to the Board within fourteen days after receiving the suspension order and the Board will make a final decision within thirty days of receiving the appeal.[99] The grounds for suspension of a license are general unlike the grounds for revocation. A license may be revoked when it failed to commence transmission within a year from the date of obtaining a license, when the license is obtained by a fraudulent process, when the broadcasting service suspends its operation for more than a month without good cause, when the licensee stops the service by its own initiative or a court orders its closure.[100] The other substantive grounds for the revocation of a license include when a transmission service violates the dignity, personal liberty and good behaviour of mankind, commits a criminal offence against the state or the government, maliciously accuses or defames individuals, peoples and organisations, and incites war.[101] And the final ground for revocation is when a broadcasting service fails to pay its license and annual fees.[102]

96. *Ibid.*, Art. 26.
97. *Ibid.*, Art. 25(1).
98. *Ibid.*, Art. 25(4).
99. *Ibid.*, Art. 28.
100. *Ibid.*, Art. 29(1) (a–e).
101. *Ibid.*, Art. 29(1) (f)).
102. *Ibid.*, Art. 29(1) (g).

Chapter 3. Programme Standards

§1. Impartiality

294. The Broadcasting Service Proclamation puts impartiality as the main programme standard for all broadcasting services. The law specifically directs the impartiality requirement to news. It says that 'every news shall be impartial, accurate and balanced'.[103] Nonetheless, impartiality is not limited to news but also to other programmes as well. This is due to the fact that the law requires any programme to reflect different and balanced viewpoints.[104] To this end, broadcasters are required to ascertain the accuracy of the content and sources of their programmes.[105]

295. While the law declares impartiality as a programme standard, it has been hardly the practice. The public broadcasting services both at the federal and regional levels have been the mouthpieces of the government. For instance, the programmes and news that are transmitted through the Ethiopian radio and television and the regional radio and television services aim to promote the good names of the government in bringing development, democracy and peace to the country. Although these public broadcasting services are transmitted in different languages, their essential purpose is not to inform the public by bringing diverse viewpoints and opinions but broadcast the works, activities, and policies of the government and the incumbent political party. The few commercial broadcasting services such as Fana Broadcasting Corporation and other commercial radio broadcasting services either support the activities and policies of the government or focus on entertainment programmes. The reason is clear. As in the print media, if the commercial broadcasters choose to be impartial and decide to channel diverse viewpoints, their life cuts short and will be coerced to shut down. Hence, there is a striking disparity between the standard of impartiality in law and in practice in the Ethiopian broadcasting landscape.

§2. Cultural Diversity

296. The issue of cultural diversity figures prominently in the broadcasting service. While there is no specific requirement that a broadcaster must consider cultural diversity in its operation, the broadcasting service law mainstreams the idea of cultural diversity as an important requirement. This is due to the fact that the public, commercial, and community broadcasting services should take into consideration the cultural diversity of their customers in their programmes. For instance, any public broadcasting service provider is obligated to present programmes that reflect

103. *Ibid.*, Art. 30(3).
104. *Ibid.*, Art. 30(1).
105. *Ibid.*, Art. 30(2).

'unity of people based on equality' and 'promote and enhance the cultural and artistic value of the public'.[106] As the Ethiopian public is culturally and linguistically diverse, the public broadcasting service is expected to transmit in different Ethiopian languages and broadcast programmes that reflect the same. Indeed, many of the public broadcasting services at the federal and regional levels transmit their news and programmes in multiple languages.

297. While the commercial broadcasting service has no such direct responsibility, the law obliges it to serve every community on an equal basis.[107] This basically configures cultural diversity into the business of commercial broadcasting. On the other hand, the issue of cultural diversity is the main subject of community broadcasters. This is because promoting and developing the culture, language and artistic values of the community is one of the main responsibility of community broadcasters.[108] Furthermore, as the broadcasting service proclamation requires national, regional and local broadcasters to spend their 60% of their weekly transmission covering national, regional and local affairs respectively,[109] they have not only a duty but also a freedom to do different programmes including those involving cultural diversity across the country, the region or the municipality.

§3. Protection of Minors

298. Under Ethiopian law, a person who is below 18 years old is a minor.[110] The broadcasting law protects children in two ways. The first is a prohibition of a radio or television to broadcast programmes that 'may corrupt the outlook of children or harm their feelings and thinking or encourage them to undesirable behavior' at hours during which children normally watch or listen to such programmes.[111] And the law sets the transmission of such programmes from 11:00 o'clock in the evening up to 5:00 o'clock in the morning as children are presumed not to listen or watch at these times.[112]

299. The second is the prohibition of any advertisement during children's programmes.[113] Children's programmes cannot be interrupted, consequently, minors are protected from targeting by business or other practices of broadcasting services.

106. *Ibid.*, Art. 16(2) (c & d).
107. *Ibid.*, 16(3) (a).
108. *Ibid.*, 16(4) (b).
109. *Ibid.*, Art. 32.
110. *See* The Ethiopian Civil Code (Negarit Gazeta 1960), Art. 198.
111. Broadcasting service proclamation, *supra* note 52, Art. 31(1).
112. *Ibid.*, Art. 31(2).
113. *Ibid.*, Art. 33(4).

§4. Human Dignity

300. The transmission of a programme that violates human dignity is prohibited and it is one of the grounds for the revocation of licence as noted above.[114] Along with human dignity, personal liberty and the good behaviour and belief of individuals are protected and broadcasters should abstain from violating any of these. The law gives a particular emphasis to the protection of the human dignity of women related to advertisements. It stipulates that 'any advertisement that violates gender equality and that disregards the dignity and human rights of women' are prohibited.[115]

§5. Right of Reply

301. The broadcasting service proclamation not only recognises the right of reply but imposes a duty to respect the right of reply to broadcasters. Article 42(1) provides that 'any broadcasting service licensee shall respect the right of a person to reply concerning an issue when the person alleges that a programme has encroached on his or her right or failed to be presented properly'. Furthermore, Article 42(2) states that the right of reply should be proportional and simultaneously with the original communication.

114. *Ibid.*, Art. 30(4).
115. *Ibid.*, Art. 34(1).

Chapter 4. Political Broadcasting

§1. Rules on Political Independence of Broadcasters

302. The Broadcasting Service Proclamation prohibits political parties from having a broadcasting licence as broadcasting should be free from political views and considerations. Article 23(3) stipulates that 'a political organisation, or an organisation of which a political organisation or a member of a political organisation's supreme leadership is a shareholder or member of its management at any level' cannot have a broadcasting license. The law even goes to the extent to prohibit the broadcasting activities of politicians who assume a higher leadership. Furthermore, public, commercial and community broadcasters are required to be impartial and independent from politics as discussed above. As a result, broadcasting services are independent from politics as a matter of law.

§2. Fair Representation in Election Periods

303. During election periods, political parties and candidates are entitled to have free airtime to promote their programmes and agendas. In this respect, Article 43 of the Broadcasting Service Proclamation stipulates that 'any broadcasting service licensee shall allocate free airtime for political organisations and candidates registered in accordance with the relevant law, to publicise their objectives and programmes to the people or to transmit statements during election period'. Accordingly, public, commercial and community broadcasters can be put to the service of political parties during election periods. Article 2(8) of this proclamation defines 'election period' as 'the period beginning from the official opening day of a campaign until 48 hours before the starting of voting day'. Hence, political parties can utilise different broadcasters to promote their electoral goals and objectives until two days from the voting day.

304. The electoral law provides that the use of mass media during election periods should be fair to all political parties. Article 59 states that 'political organisations and sections of the community that are in support of a candidate shall be entitled to equal access to state owned mass media including radio, TV and newspapers'. It also stipulates that such use of the media is for free. Similarly, Article 9(4) of the EBC proclamation imposes a duty on the EBA to ensure that political parties are given balanced radio and television airtime. Indeed, this duty is not limited to an election period but will be critically important in this period. While the law imposes a duty to all broadcasters to give free and fair airtime to political parties and individual candidates during an election, the public service broadcasting assumes more obligation in this respect.

§3. News and Current Affairs Programmes

305. Although there is no general obligation or duty on all broadcasters to cover news and activities of political parties outside an election period, public service broadcasters assume a special obligation. Article 16(2(c)) of the broadcasting service proclamation imposes a duty on public service broadcasters to serve political parties on the basis of equality. This means that they have to do news and cover stories about the activities and actions of political parties when they do some activities. However, commercial and community broadcasters do not have such obligation unless they choose so.

§4. Political Advertising

306. Political parties and individual candidates are entitled to make election campaign advertisements. Article 2(6) of the broadcasting service proclamation defines election campaign advertisement as 'a radio or television message conveyed by a political organisation or candidate to publicise about himself and his aspirations by paying or promising to pay for the announcement'. In addition to the free airtime from different broadcasters, political parties or individual candidates can do election campaign advertisements. In election campaign advertisements, the political party or the individual candidate making the campaign is responsible for the legality and the substance of the advertisement. When advertising, broadcasters cannot collect a fee more than they collect from commercial advertisements and nor can discriminate among political parties or candidates.

307. Political advertising is done during an election period and political parties or candidates cannot advertise outside of this period. The electoral law protects political advertising. Any removal of such advertisements is a punishable criminal offence. Article 99 of the electoral law stipulates the following in this regard: 'Whosoever has, from the commencement of the election process up to the official announcement of results, damaged, removed or torn apart a poster or election advertisement of any candidate shall be punishable with imprisonment not exceeding one year or a fine.'

Chapter 5. Advertising Rules

§1. Various Forms of Commercial Communications

308. The public and the commercial broadcasting services are the main platforms for commercial communications. The public broadcasting service, in particular, the Ethiopian radio and television are the major channels of commercial broadcasting. This has partly to do with the governments sole ownership of broadcasting services for much of its operation and the concomitant consolidation of the public broadcasting service in terms of coverage and technologies. Some commercial broadcasting services, specifically those operating in Addis Ababa, are also major forms of commercial communications in particular related to entertainment.

309. Advertisements and sponsorship programmes are the main means of commercial advertisements. Article 2(5) of the Broadcasting Service Proclamation defines advertisements as 'a message transmitted to publicise and promote sales of goods and services'. In a similar suit, Article 2(7) defines sponsored programmes as 'a programme the transmission cost of which is paid directly or indirectly or the payment of which is promised'.

310. Article 33 of the Broadcasting Proclamation provides the general rule of advertisements. Article 33(1) provides that advertisements should be transmitted in a manner that clearly differentiates them from other programmes and should not affect the content of other programmes. Article 33(2) requires a commercial advertisement to be truthful, not misleading and lawful. Article 33(3) prohibits the transmission of malicious or undermining advertisement on the products or services of others, while Article 33(4) prohibits that commercial or any other advertisements interrupt the transmission of any programme the time of which is not more than twenty minutes or children's programmes. Nonetheless, there is an exception to the rule of non-interruption in case of emergency. In this regard, Article 41 provides that 'any broadcasting service licensee shall transmit, free of charge, emergency statements given by the federal or a regional state government due to the occurrence of an incident that endangers the constitutional order of the country, a natural disaster or an epidemic that threatens public health'. As emergency is an unexpected state of affairs, its occurrence can interrupt the transmission of other advertisements or programmes. However, for other government statements, broadcasters can charge advertisement fees and the standard rules apply.[116]

§2. Restrictions on Content

311. Article 34 provides the following restrictions on advertisements:

116. *Ibid.*, Art. 41(2).

- any advertisement that violates gender equality and that disregards the dignity and human rights of women;
- cigarette and cigarette-related advertisements;
- advertisements related to narcotic drugs;
- advertisements of liquors with more than 12% alcoholic contents;
- advertisements that encourage users to buy medicine that cannot be obtained without medical prescription; and
- other advertisements prohibited by law.

§3. Time and Frequency Restrictions

312. As to the time and frequency of advertisements, Article 35 of the Broadcasting Service Proclamation provides two rules. The first is if the broadcasting service is an advertisement station, there is no restriction on the time and frequency of the advertisement. Put differently, the law hints for the operation of purely advertising broadcasting services. However, if it is not an advertising station, any broadcasting station shall not allocate more than 20% of its daily transmission or in a particular programme time to advertisements.

§4. Sponsorship

313. Article 36 governs sponsorship programmes. It provides that sponsorship programmes shall be free from the influence of the sponsor. In this respect, Article 36(1) states that the content and timetable of a sponsored programme neither shall fall under the influence of the sponsor nor shall agitate the sale or hire of the sponsor's products or services. Furthermore, not everyone is entitled to sponsor a programme. Article 36(2) excludes those businesses who produce or sell goods or render services for which advertising is prohibited by law from being sponsors.

314. Article 36(3) stipulates that sponsorship programmes should not be interrupted by other commercial advertisements. However, the law gives freedom to the sponsor and the station to agree otherwise. Thus, it is a default rule. Article 36(4) requires the station to announce the name of the sponsor at least at the beginning and end of the sponsored programme.

§5. Product Placement

315. The Broadcasting Proclamation does not provide rules for product placement.

Chapter 6. Right to Information

§1. Access to Major Events

316. While the broadcasting proclamation aspires to enforce access to information, it did not stipulate access to major events as a right of broadcasters. As a result, access to major events, in particular to commercial broadcasters, is at the discretion of the government or the organiser of the event.

§2. Short News Reporting

317. However, the law requires any broadcaster to cover national and regional news in its programmes.[117] Accordingly, broadcasters should report short news including major events. This may entitle them to access those events. Nonetheless, short news reporting is rather a duty than a right for broadcasters.

117. *Ibid.*, Art. 16(3) (c).

Chapter 7. Access to Networks

§1. Must Carry Rules

318. The Broadcasting Proclamation imposes some 'must carry rules' on public, commercial and community broadcasting services:

(1) Article 16(2) provides the following related to public broadcasting services:
   (a) enhance the participation of the public through the presentation of government policies and strategies as well as activities related to development, democracy and good governance;
   (b) present programmes which inform, educate and entertain the public;
   (c) present programmes which reflect unity of peoples based on equality;
   (d) promote and enhance the cultures and artistic values of the public;
   (e) serve political parties operating in accordance with the Constitution and the electoral laws of the country on the basis of fair and just treatment.
(2) According to Article 16(3), commercial broadcasting services must:
   (a) provide equal treatment to any community in its license area;
   (b) transmission of its programmes shall cover the whole area of its license;
   (c) include regional and national news in its programmes;
   (d) submit to register the license given by the authority to the Ministry of Trade and Industry or to the Regional Trade and Industry Bureau.
(3) Article 16(4) obliges community broadcasting services to:
   (a) carry out their activities based on the needs of the community regarding development, education and good governance;
   (b) promote and develop the language, culture and artistic value of the community;
   (c) allow the participation of the members of the community in the preparation of their programmes;
   (d) transmit programmes on issues involving the common interests of the community that could not get coverage by other broadcasting services;
   (e) utilise the income derived from different sources for the operation of the broadcasting station;
   (f) provide community centered informative and entertaining programmes to promote the information culture and knowledge of the community.

§2. Other Access Obligations for Networks

319. There are no other access obligations for networks in Ethiopia.

Chapter 8. Standards and Interoperability

320. The Broadcasting Proclamation does not provide detailed rule on standards and interoperability. Instead, it gives power to the EBA to set standards for broadcasting services. The EBA has the power to:

(a) determine the type and standard of equipment to be used for a broadcasting service as well as the capacity of the transmitter;[118]
(b) control illegal transmissions;[119]
(c) plan, permit and control the use of the radio wave allocated for broadcasting services by the concerned organ and lease the use of the radio wave;[120]
(d) prescribe technical standards for different categories of broadcasting services;[121]
(e) prescribe standards for broadcasting equipment; issue certificates of compliance to importers of the instruments and supervise their operations.[122]

321. In addition, the EBA can provide standard requirements in issuing a license.[123]

118. *Ibid.*, Art. 7(4).
119. *Ibid.*, Art. 7(5).
120. *Ibid.*, Art. 7(6).
121. *Ibid.*, Art. 7(8).
122. *Ibid.*, Art. 7(9).
123. *Ibid.*, Art. 21.

Part IV. Cross Ownership Regulation

322. Article 7 of the Press Proclamation deals with media ownership:

(1) Any person who exercises direct or indirect effective control over a company possessing a nation-wide broadcasting license or a broadcasting license for an area with a recorded population of more than 100,000 inhabitants, may not exercise direct or indirect effective control over another company holding such a license and serving the same or an overlapping market.
(2) Any person who exercises direct or indirect effective control over a company holding a nation-wide license or a license for an area with a recorded population of more than 100,000 inhabitants may not exercise direct or indirect effective control over a company operating a periodical serving the same or an overlapping market.
(3) Without prejudice to (1) and (2) of this Article any person who exercises effective direct or indirect control over a company operating a periodical may not exercise effective direct or indirect control over another company running a periodical published in the same language and serving the same or an overlapping market.
(4) The procedure for determining and assessing effective control, referred to in (1)–(3) of this Article, shall be laid down by specific law, in the absence of evidence to the contrary, a person shall be regarded as exercising such control if he either directly or indirectly holds 15% or more of the shares or capital of the entity.

323. This Article prohibits cross ownership of both the print and broadcast media. In addition, financial control or share is only one element in assessing effective control in the regulation of media ownership.

Part V. Supervision: Media Regulator

Chapter 1. Organisation

324. The Ministry of Information, now Ministry for Communication Office, is the government entity responsible for media regulation in Ethiopia. However, the regulation of print and broadcasting media is not the same. With respect to the print media, the Ministry for Communications Office directly regulates it. Article 9 of the Press Proclamation provides that anyone who desires to publish a periodical shall register it with the Ministry of Communication Office if the distribution goes beyond one regional state, and with the Communication Bureau of the region if the proposed distribution is limited to one regional state.

325. With regard to broadcasting media, however, a special organisation is established as a regulator under the accountability of the Ministry of Communication Office. Article 4 of the Broadcasting Proclamation establishes the EBA as a broadcasting service regulator under the supervision of the Ministry of Communication Office. As stated in Article 8 of the Broadcasting Proclamation, the EBA is constituted of a Board, Director General, Deputy Director General and the necessary staff. Members of the Board are drawn from different institutions and parts of the society and are appointed by the Government on the recommendation of the Ministry of Communication Office.[124] The number of members of the Board is also determined by the Government.[125] The Director General should be a member and secretary of the Board.[126] The Board is accountable to the Ministry of Communication Office.[127]

326. Both the Director General and the Deputy Director General of EBA are appointed by the Government upon recommendation by the Ministry of Communications Office.[128]

124. *Ibid.*, Art. 9(2).
125. *Ibid.*, Art. 9(1).
126. *Ibid.*, Art. 9(3).
127. *Ibid.*, Art. 9(4).
128. *Ibid.*, Arts 12(1) & 13(1).

Chapter 2. Tasks

327. Article 10 of the Broadcasting Proclamation provides the tasks and powers of the Board. These are:

(1) overseeing the implementation of the Broadcasting Proclamation and the activities of EBA;
(2) reviewing the annual work programmes and budgets as well as the activity reports of EBA;
(3) reviewing and submitting to the Ministry of Communications Office, for its approval, directives to be issued for the implementation of the Broadcasting Proclamation;
(4) examining and deciding on complaints brought by applicants and licensees; examining and deciding on appeals on decisions given against broadcasters on the basis of public complaints;
(5) deliberating and, as may be appropriate, deciding on policy matters pertaining to the implementation of the Broadcasting Proclamation.

328. In order to perform these tasks, the Board shall meet once a month; however, the chairperson can arrange extra meetings when necessary.[129] The Board decides by majority vote and presence of more than half of its members constitute a quorum.[130] In case of a tie, the chairperson has a casting vote.[131]

329. As stipulated in Article 12 of the Broadcasting Proclamation, the Director General is the Chief Executive of the EBA and shall direct and administer its activities subject to the general directive of the Board. Furthermore, the Director General is able to exercise the powers and perform the duties of EBA provided in Article 7 of the Broadcasting Proclamation.[132] These powers and duties are to:

(1) ensure that the broadcasting service is conducted in such a manner that contributes to the proper social, economic, political and cultural development of the country;
(2) issue, suspend and cancel broadcasting service licenses;
(3) determine the site and coverage area of a broadcasting station to avoid an overlap with any radio communication;
(4) determine the type and standard of equipment to be used for a broadcasting service as well as the capacity of the transmitter;
(5) control illegal transmissions;
(6) plan, permit and control the use of the radio wave allocated for broadcasting service by the concerned organ and lease the use of the radio wave;
(7) conduct study with regard to the development and improvement of the broadcasting services; compile and maintain information related to the services;

129. *Ibid.*, Art. 11(1).
130. *Ibid.*, Art. 11(2 & 3).
131. *Ibid.*, Art. 11(3).
132. *Ibid.*, Art. 12(3) (a).

(8) prescribe technical standards for different categories of broadcasting services;
(9) prescribe standards for broadcasting equipment; issue certificates of compliance to importers of the instruments and supervise their operations;
(10) decide on complaints arising in relation to broadcasting services;
(11) without prejudice to the relevant laws and government directives participate, on behalf of the government, in international meetings on matters related to broadcasting services; follow up the implementation of international agreements on broadcasting services to which the country is a party;
(12) fix and collect license fees for broadcasting services;
(13) pay the appropriate fee for the radio wave allocated by the concerned organ;

330. In addition, Article 12 confers the following tasks and powers to the Director General:

– appointing and administering employees of the Authority in accordance with directives to be approved by the government following the basic principles of the federal civil service laws;
– preparing and submitting to the Board the work programme and budget of the Authority, and implementing the work programme when approved by the appropriate organ;
– effecting expenditure in accordance with the work programme and budget of the EBA;
– representing the EBA in all its dealings with third parties;
– preparing and submitting to the Board the activity and financial reports of the EBA.

331. The Deputy Director General, subject to the supervision of the Director General, directs and co-ordinates units placed under his supervision and performs other activities assigned to him by the Director General.

Chapter 3. Sanctioning Powers

332. The EBA has sanctioning powers ranging from imposing fines for a delayed payment of license and annual fees, to suspension and revocation of licence for violating the Broadcasting Proclamation.[133] The EBA can also impose a penal punishment through fines. The fines vary according to the violation. Article 45 provides the following with regard to fines; Unless punishable with a more severe penalty under the Criminal Code, any person found guilty of violating:

- Article 18 of this [Broadcasting] Proclamation shall be punishable with a fine not less than Birr 50,000 and not exceeding Birr 100,000;
- Sub-Article (1), (2) or (3) of Article 30 of this Proclamation shall be punishable with a fine not less than Birr 10,000 and not exceeding Birr 50,000;
- Article 31 of this Proclamation shall be punishable with a fine not less than Birr 10,000 and not exceeding Birr 25,000;
- Article 33(3) or 34 of this Proclamation shall be punishable with a fine not less than Birr 20,000 and not exceeding Birr 30,000;
- Sub-Article (1), (2) or (4) of Article 33, Article 35 or 36 of this Proclamation shall be given a warning in writing for the first violation, and be punishable with a fine not less than Birr 5,000 and not exceeding Birr 10,000 for the second violation;
- Article 37 or 39 of this Proclamation shall be given a warning in writing for the first violation, and be punishable with a fine not less than Birr 5,000 and not exceeding Birr 15,000 for the second violation;
- Article 39 or 43 of this Proclamation shall be punishable with a fine not less than Birr 20,000 and not exceeding Birr 50,000.

333. In addition, Article 46 stipulates that the property of a broadcaster shall, in addition to the principal penalty, be confiscated if that broadcaster is found, in accordance with the provisions of the relevant criminal law, guilty of violating the provision of Article 30(4) of the Broadcasting Proclamation.

133. *Ibid.*, Arts 27(2), 28 & 29.

Selected Bibliography

Aalen, L. & K. Tronvoll. 'The 2008 Ethiopian Local Elections: The Return of Electoral Authoritarianism'. *African Affairs* 108, no. 430 (2008): 111-120.

Abebe, A.K. *Rule by Law in Ethiopia: Rendering Constitutional Limits on Government Power Nonsensical*, CGHR Working Paper 1, Cambridge: University of Cambridge Centre of Governance and Human Rights, April 2012.

Abebe, A.K. *The Potential Role of Constitutional Review in the Realization of Human Rights in Ethiopia*, LLD Thesis, University of Pretoria, 2012.

Abraha, H.H. 'Examining Approaches to Internet Regulation in Ethiopia'. *Information & Communications Technology Law* 26, no. 3 (2017), DOI: 10.1080/13600834.2017.1374057, 1-20.

Alemu, G. & S. Alemahu. *The Constitutional Protection of Human Rights in Ethiopia: Challenges and Prospects*. Addis Ababa: Faculty of Law, Addis Ababa University, 2008.

Ali, M.S. 'Jurisprudential Challenges to Freedom of Expression in Ethiopia: Critical Reflections on Selected Legislations of the Country'. *The Internet Journal Language, Culture and Society* 42 (2016): 1-12. URL: http://aaref.com.au/en/publications/journal/ISSN 1327-774X (accessed 1 July 2017).

Aliyi, K. *Ethiopian Media Industry: Ownership and Regulations from a Historical Point of View*, M.A Thesis, Addis Ababa University, 2013.

Arriola, L.R. & T. Lyons. 'Ethiopia: The 100% Election'. *Journal of Democracy* 27, no. 1 (2016): 76-88.

Barak-Erez, D. & D. Scharia. 'Freedom of Speech, Support for Terrorism, and the Challenge of Global Constitutional Law'. *Harvard National Security Journal* 2, no. 1 (2011): 1-30.

Boyne, S.M. 'Free Speech, Terrorism, and European Security: Defining and Defending the Political Community'. Pace Law Review 30, no. 2 (2009/10): 417-483.

Brems, E. 'Ethiopia Before the United Nations Treaty Monitoring Bodies'. *Africa Focus* 20, no. 1-2 (2007): 49-74.

Clapham, C. 'Post-War Ethiopia: The Trajectories of Crisis'. *Review of African Political Economy* 36, no. 120 (2009): 181-192.

Dejene, M. 'The Role of the Private Print Media in the Post-Socialist Ethiopia: Views from Government, Opposition Politicians, Academics and the Private Press'. *Global Media Journal African Edition* 7, no. 2 (2013): 140-171.

Dirbaba, B.O. 'Silent Censor: The Influence of Authoritarian Family Socialization on Professional Journalism in Ethiopia'. *Journalism* (2015): 1-19.

Selected Bibliography

Dirbaba, B.O. & P. O'Donnell. 'The Double Talk of Manipulative Liberalism in Ethiopia: An Example of New Strategies of Media Repression'. *African Communication Research* 3, no. (2) (2012): 283-312.

Donald N. Levine, *Greater Ethiopia: The Evolution of a Multiethnic Society.* Chicago: University of Chicago Press, 2000.

Etana, A. *The Status and Descent of Press Freedom in Ethiopia: Factors That Account.* Ethiopia: Addis Ababa University, 2014.

Fasil Nahum, *Constitution for a Nation of Nations: The Ethiopian Prospect.* Asmara: The Red Sea Press, 1997.

Faris, E.B. *The Impact of Party Dominance on the Role of Parliamentary Oversight for the Protection of Human Rights in Ethiopia.* Cape Town: The University of Western Cape, Faculty of Law, 2012.

Fojo Media Institute. *Strengthening Free, Independent and Professional Journalism in Ethiopia: Feasibility Study.* Addis Ababa/Stockholm: Linnaeus University, August 2017.

Gezahegn, R. *Political Criticism and Defamatory Speech: Ethiopian Law in Comparative Context*, July 2017. Available at: https://dokupdf.com/download/-political-criticism-and-defamatory-speech-ethiopian-law-in-comparative-context-_5a01dbb7d64ab2b9bd79f71f_pdf (accessed 22 March 2018).

Gudina, M. 'Elections and Democratization in Ethiopia: 1991–2010'. *Journal of Eastern African Studies* 5, no. 4 (2011): 664-680.

Harbeson, J.W. 'Election and Democratization in Post-Mengistu Ethiopia'. In *Post-Conflict Elections, Democratization, and International Assistance*, edited by Kumar et al. Boulder, Colorado: Lynne Rienner, 1998.

Justin, L. (eds). 'Ethiopia'. In *Media Law Handbook for Eastern Africa – Volume 1*, Johannesburg: Konrad-Adenauer-Stiftung Regional Media Programme, 2016, 213-293.

Kibret, Z. 'The Terrorism of Counter-Terrorism: The Use and Abuse of Anti-Terrorism Law, the Case of Ethiopia'. *European Scientific Journal* 13 (2017): 504-539.

Lencho, N. *Media and Communication for Development and Democratization in Ethiopia: Journalistic Practices and Challenges.* Published Ph.d. thesis, Addis Ababa University, 2010.

Lyons, T. 'Ethiopian Elections: Past and Future'. *International Journal of Ethiopian Studies* 5, no. 1(2010): 107-121.

Lyons, T. *The Puzzle of Ethiopia: From Rebel Victory to Authoritarian Politics (1991-2015).* Boulder Colo: Lynne Reiner, 2017.

Mekonen, D.Y. 'Assessing Controversial Issues of the Ethiopian Anti-Terrorism Law: A Special Focus on Substantive Matters'. *Journal of Law, Policy & Globalization* (2015): 40.

Mengistu, Y.L. 'Shielding Marginalised Groups from Verbal Assaults'. In *The Content and Context of Hate Speech: Rethinking Regulation and Responses*, edited by M. Herz & P. Molnar.Cambridge: Cambridge University Press, 2012.

O'Flaherty, M. 'Freedom of Expression: Article 19 of the International Covenant on Civil and Political Rights and the Human Rights Committee's General Comment No. 34'. *Human Rights Law Review* 12, no. 3 (2012): 627-654.

ÓLoughlin, C. & P. Schafraad. 'News on the Move: Towards a Typology of Journalists in Exile'. *Observatorio* 10, no. 1 (2016): 45-66.

Ross, T.J. 'A test of democracy: Ethiopia's Mass Media and Freedom of Information Proclamation'. *Penn State Law Review* 114, no. 3 (2010): 1047-1066.

Sekyere, P. & B. Asare. 'An Examination of Ethiopia's Anti-Terrorism Proclamation on Fundamental Human Rights'. *European Scientific Journal* 12, no. 1 (2016): 351-371.

Skjerdal, T. *Competing Loyalties: Journalism Culture in Ethiopian State Media*, Ph.d. Dissertation, University of Oslo, 2012.

Skjerdal, T. *Journalists in Ethiopia: Country Report*, NLA University College, Worlds of Journalism Study, 20 October, 2016.

Skjerdal, T.S. & H. Lule. 'Uneven Performances by the Private Press in Ethiopia: An Analysis of 18 Years of Press Freedom'. *Journal of Communication and Language Arts* 3, no. 1 (2009): 44-59.

Skjerdal, T.S. 'Development Journalism Revived: The Case of Ethiopia'. *Eciquid Novi: African Journalism Studies* 32, no. 2 (2011): 58-74.

Skjerdal, T.S. 'Online Journalism under Pressure: An Ethiopian Account'. In *Online Journalism in Africa: Trends, Practices and Emerging Cultures*, edited by J. Whittaker, H.M. Mabweazara & O.F. Mudhai. New York: Routledge, 2013.

Skjerdal, T.S. 'Why the Arab Spring Never Came to Ethiopia'. In *Participatory Politics and Citizen Journalism in a Networked Africa*, edited by B. Mutsvairo. London: Palgrave Macmillan, 2016.

Smith, L. *Political Violence and Democratic Uncertainty in Ethiopia*, United States Institute of Peace, Special Report No. 192, August 2007.

Stremlau, N. 'Media, Participation and Constitution-Making in Ethiopia'. *Journal of African Law* 58, no. 2 (2014): 231-249.

Stremlau, N. 'The Press and the Political Restructuring of Ethiopia'. *Journal of Eastern African Studies* 5, no. 4 (2011): 716-732.

Tadeg, M.A. 'Freedom of Expression and the Media Landscape in Ethiopia: Contemporary Challenges'. *UB Journal of Media Law & Ethics* 5, no. 1/2, (2016): 69-99.

Tesfaye, A., *Social Media as an Alternative Political Forum in Ethiopia: The Case of Face book.* Unpublished MA thesis, Addis Ababa University, School of Journalism and Communication, 2013.

Timothewos, G. 'Freedom of Expression in Ethiopia: The Jurisprudential Dearth'. *Mizan Law Review* 4, no. 2 (2010): 201-231.

Selected Bibliography

Index

The numbers here refer to paragraph numbers.

Index